THE ULTIMATE MUSICIAN'S PRACTICE PLANNER

Progress Journal & Theory Reference

Brent Robitaille

KALYMI MUSIC
brentrobitaille.com

OTHER BOOKS BY BRENT ROBITAILLE

- Beginner Guitar Chord Book
- The Pop Rock Looper Pedal Book
- The Blues Guitar Looper Pedal Book
- The Jazz Guitar Looper Pedal Book
- DADGAD Guitar Tuning - Celtic Flatpicking
- Open D Guitar Tuning - Celtic Collection
- Open G Guitar Tuning - Celtic Flatpicking
- Classical Guitar Book in Open D Tuning
- The Open D Christmas Songbook
- Improve Your Guitar Chord Playing
- The Slide Guitar Collection
- Mandolin Blues Book
- Celtic Mandola Book
- Celtic Collection for Mandolin
- Easy Classical Violin Tabs
- Fiddle Tab - Celtic Collection
- Holiday Collection for Fiddle Tab
- Traditional Collection FiddleTab
- 101 Blues Guitar Riffs & Solos in Open D
- 101 Blues Guitar Riffs & Solos in Open G
- Mastering Ukulele Fingerstyle
- Celtic Collection for Ukulele
- The Ukulele Christmas Songbook
- Ultimate Ukulele Technique & WarmUp Book
- Ukulele Blank Tab Collection and Reference Book
- Cigar Box Guitar - Jazz & Blues Unlimited Series
- Ultimate Collection – Cigar Box Guitar Vol. 1 & 2
- Mandolin Blank Tab Collection & Reference Book
- Cigar Box Guitar - Classical Collection
- Cigar Box Guitar Blues Overload
- 101 Riffs for Cigar Box Guitar
- Celtic Collection for Cigar Box Guitar
- Cigar Box Guitar - The Technique Book
- Holiday Collection for Cigar Box Guitar
- Complete Cigar Box Guitar Chord Book
- Country & Bluegrass Cigar Box Guitar Book
- The Celtic Resonator Guitar Book
- Piano Grooves Volume 1
- The Complete Guitarist Practice Planner
- The Ultimate Musician's Practice Planner

A very special thank you to Katelyn Robitaille for her excellent contribution to the design of the Creative Reset pages. And, as always, to my wife and co-editor, Cathy Robitaille, and my entire family for their unwavering support!

Audio - Video - Ebooks - Sheet Music
www.brentrobitaille.com

KALYMI MUSIC

PUBLISHED BY KALYMI MUSIC
©2025 Kalymi Music

Although the author and publisher have made every effort to ensure that the information in this book is in public domain at press time, the author and publisher do not assume and hereby disclaim any liability to any party. Any copying of this material whole or in part with the express written permission of Kalymi Publishing is a violation of copyright law.

The Ultimate Musician's Practice Planner

INTRODUCTION

I created The Ultimate Musician's Practice Planner to solve two common challenges I saw repeatedly: musicians often practice without a clear sense of direction or progress, and performing musicians become so focused on preparing for gigs that consistent, skill-building practice gets pushed aside.

This system is the framework I wish I had when balancing studio sessions, class assignments, and consistent skill practice.

It transforms scattered effort into a focused, integrated approach, allowing you to **stop chasing loose notes and start achieving measurable results.**

ABOUT THE AUTHOR

Brent Robitaille is a Canadian composer, educator, and the founder of Kalymi Music Publishing. His professional foundation is built on intensive studies at **McGill University, York University,** and the **Royal Conservatory of Music**.

His work integrates high-level academic training, including a co-authored publication in the Empirical Studies of the Arts, with extensive professional experience, including recording on numerous albums, work in television, and years of performing experience.

After decades of teaching musicians of all ages, Brent recognized a common challenge: players were practicing, but lacked a clear system to guide their progress. This realization became the starting point for this planner. Blending his expertise from the concert hall to the classroom, Brent structured this book as a reliable, organized tool encompassing goal-setting, practice logs, performance tracking, and theory reference. His objective is simple: to help players improve steadily, maintain focus, and make every practice session meaningful.

How This Planner is Set Up:

(Foundations and Setup)

CORE
1. **Daily** Practice Session Tracker
2. **Weekly** Practice Summary and Teacher / Lesson Notes
3. **Monthly** Reflection & Creative Reset

(Theory and Reference)

(Creative Notes and Manuscript)

Overview of Each Section

Foundations and Setup
Start with planning pages to set clear goals and stay organized.

- SOUND Goal Framework
- Master Practice Goal Planner:
- Repertoire Master List
- Technique & Skill Development
- Creative Works Master List
- Gigs and Performance Log
- Gear and Setup Log
- Blank Calendar for lessons, rehearsals, and performances

Daily Practice Session
Use this page every time you sit down to practice.

- Today's Focus
- How long you practiced
- What you practiced (playing, technique, creativity, projects)
- Improvements you noticed
- Areas that need more work
- A quick reflection on how the session felt
- Your next focus for the following session

Weekly Practice Summary

After several daily sessions, complete a weekly summary.

- List your top accomplishments
- Identify what you worked on most
- Record what improved
- Identify what needs more attention
- Choose your focus for the next week

Teacher and Lesson Notes

Use this page if you take lessons or want a record of outside guidance.

- Assignments
- Recommended practice time
- Repertoire to prepare
- Teacher comments
- Student notes

Monthly Review

At the end of each month, take a few minutes to reflect.

- Set longer-term goals
- Evaluate goals you want to continue
- Record the biggest lessons or breakthroughs
- Give yourself a monthly progress rating

Theory and Reference

This section contains the theory charts you reach for most often.

- Key Signatures • Circle of Fifths • Chord Formulas/Inversions
- Mode Reference Guide • Improvisation Map & Scales
- Interval and Keyboard Charts • Rhythm and Time Signatures
- Instrument Ranges • Transposition • Figured Bass and the Nashville Number System

Creative Notes and Manuscript

The final pages give you room to think, write, and create.

- Lined and Manuscript
- Blank Manuscript Pages
- Essential Music Glossary
- Music History Quick Reference

TABLE OF CONTENTS

Introduction 3
How to Use This Planner 4
Musician Snapshot 7

FOUNDATIONS & SETUP

SOUND Goal Framework & Master Practice Goal Planner 8
Repertoire Master List 10
Technique & Skill Development Master List 12
Creative Works Master List 14
Gigs & Performance Log 16
Gear & Setup Log 18
Master Notes & Projects 20
Blank Calendar 22

THE PRACTICE SYSTEM (Based on a 28 Day Cycle)

| Daily-Weekly | ⟶ | Daily-Weekly-Teacher | x4 | Monthly-Creative | x1 |

The Practice System .... 28 - 207
End of Season Review 208

THEORY & REFERENCE

Integrated Theory and Reference Introduction 209
Key Signatures 210
Circle of Fifths 211
Chord Formulas & Spelling Guide 212
Major & Minor Inversions 214
Master Reference Scale Chart 215
Mode Reference Guide 216
Improvisation Map 217
Interval & Keyboard Charts 218
Figured Bass & Nashville Number System 219
Instrument Ranges 220
Standard Transposing Instrument Reference Chart 221
Time Signatures & Rhythm Charts 222

CREATIVE & NOTES SECTION

Music History Quick Reference 224
Essential Music Glossary 226
Creative Ideas (Lined) 229
Blank Manuscript Pages 234
Ideas & Notes (Lined + Manuscript) 238

MUSICIAN SNAPSHOT

Name: _____

Primary Instrument: _____

Start Date: _____

Current Strengths:

_____
_____
_____
_____
_____

Current Weak Spots:

_____
_____
_____
_____
_____

12-Month Musical Goal:

_____
_____
_____
_____
_____

"The best way to predict the future is to create it." – Peter Drucker

Introduction to the S.O.U.N.D. Framework

The S.O.U.N.D. Framework is a musician-focused adaptation of the S.M.A.R.T. goals system.

After years of teaching, I realized the greatest obstacle to progress wasn't a lack of talent; it was a **lack of focus.** Students were pulled in too many directions at once. They struggled to articulate goals clearly, and lacked the simple structure needed to make real progress. My job was to help them concentrate on one thing at a time.

I developed this framework to move beyond theory and provide a practical checklist for success. Students understand goal setting but struggle to apply it in practice.

Why S.O.U.N.D. Works

The S.O.U.N.D. Framework removes the guesswork, helping you shape clear, focused, and realistic goals. It works because it mirrors the natural way musicians learn: **step by step, sound by sound.**

You can apply S.O.U.N.D. throughout this planner. When your goals are **Simple, Observable, Useful, Natural, and Dated**, you stop drifting and begin following a clear, workable path. Use this framework consistently, and your practice will become more organized, leading to steady, reliable musical growth.

S – **Simple:** Keep it simple; focus on one task at a time to avoid multitasking.

O – **Observable:** Track your progress and ask: "Am I improving?"

U – **Useful:** Question what you are practicing: "How is this useful?"

N – **Natural:** Choose goals that match your long-term musical direction.

D – **Dated:** Set a specific target or review date to complete a task.

Master Practice Goal Planner

   Before you begin the core sections of this planner (the daily practice session, weekly summary, and monthly reflection pages), use these opening charts and logs to establish and define your long-term goals for the year. There are six core categories I use that will give you a clear place to return to as you refine your focus and maintain year-long progress.

1. Repertoire Master List
Use this chart to track your main pieces and studies over the year. Note when you began working on each item, what you're focusing on, and how it's progressing. This helps you stay organized and see your development more clearly.

2. Technique & Skill Development Master List
Technique can mean many things. It includes the technical work we often think of, like scales, arpeggios, patterns, and drills, but it also refers to developing the physical skills behind your playing—tone, control, timing, coordination, and ease of movement. Use this section to choose the specific skills you want to strengthen over the year and track how they improve.

3. Creative Works Master List
Use this page to track your songs, riffs, sketches, and musical ideas. Note where they're stored, what they're for, and any musical details so you can return to them and develop them over time.

4. Gigs & Performances Log
Use this page to keep track of upcoming gigs and performances, along with the essential details you need to stay prepared. Record the date, venue, setlist notes, gear requirements, and any important reminders so every performance runs smoothly.

5. Gear & Setup Log
Use this page to document your instrument setup, gear settings, maintenance notes, and technical preferences. These entries help you stay consistent from one session or performance to the next, and make it easier to recreate your best sounds.

6. Master Notes & Projects
Use this page to track the long-term projects and insights that shape your year. Write down anything you want to remember, develop, or return to later. This is your space for the important ideas that don't fit anywhere else.

♪ Repertoire Master List ♪

Use this log to keep track of all your current pieces, technique, and studies.

#	Title	Composer	Date	Tempo	Notes / Focus Area
1					
2					
3					
4					
5					
6					
7					
8					
9					
10					
11					
12					

♪ Repertoire Master List ♪

Use this log to keep track of all your current pieces, technique, and studies.

#	Title	Composer	Date	Tempo	Notes / Focus Area
1					
2					
3					
4					
5					
6					
7					
8					
9					
10					
11					
12					

🎵 Technique & Skill Development Master List 🎵

Track the technical skills and exercises you want to improve this year.

#	Exercise / Skill	Technical Focus	Tempo	Date	Progress
1					
2					
3					
4					
5					
6					
7					
8					
9					
10					
11					
12					

🎵 Technique & Skill Development Master List 🎵

Track the technical skills and exercises you want to improve this year.

#	Exercise / Skill	Technical Focus	Tempo	Date	Progress
1					
2					
3					
4					
5					
6					
7					
8					
9					
10					
11					
12					

🎵 Creative Works Master List 🎵

Use this page to capture musical ideas you want to develop over time.

Title / Idea	Type	Status	Purpose	Notes	Date

🎵 Creative Works Master List 🎵

Use this page to capture musical ideas you want to develop over time.

Title / Idea	Type	Status	Purpose	Notes	Date

Gigs & Performances

Keep track of upcoming gigs and performances with the essential details.

Date	Time	Venue/Contact	Gear	Performance Notes

Gigs & Performances

Keep track of upcoming gigs and performances with the essential details.

Date	Time	Venue/Contact	Gear	Performance Notes

Gear & Setup Log

Track your instruments and setups to maintain a consistent sound.

Instrument	Setup	Gear	Tuning	Notes & Maintenance

Gear & Setup Log
Track your instruments and setups to maintain a consistent sound.

Instrument	Setup	Gear	Tuning	Notes & Maintenance

MASTER NOTES & PROJECTS

Use this chart to remember long-term projects, key insights, and ideas.

Project / Topic	Purpose	Action	Resources	Notes	Date

MASTER NOTES & PROJECTS

Use this chart to remember long-term projects, key insights, and ideas.

Project / Topic	Purpose	Action	Resources	Notes	Date

BLANK CALENDAR - Check all important dates, exams, and performance goals here.

#	JANUARY	#	FEBRUARY
1		1	
2		2	
3		3	
4		4	
5		5	
6		6	
7		7	
8		8	
9		9	
10		10	
11		11	
12		12	
13		13	
14		14	
15		15	
16		16	
17		17	
18		18	
19		19	
20		20	
21		21	
22		22	
23		23	
24		24	
25		25	
26		26	
27		27	
28		28	
29		29	
30			
31			

MARCH		APRIL	
1		1	
2		2	
3		3	
4		4	
5		5	
6		6	
7		7	
8		8	
9		9	
10		10	
11		11	
12		12	
13		13	
14		14	
15		15	
16		16	
17		17	
18		18	
19		19	
20		20	
21		21	
22		22	
23		23	
24		24	
25		25	
26		26	
27		27	
28		28	
29		29	
30		30	
31			

MAY		JUNE	
1		1	
2		2	
3		3	
4		4	
5		5	
6		6	
7		7	
8		8	
9		9	
10		10	
11		11	
12		12	
13		13	
14		14	
15		15	
16		16	
17		17	
18		18	
19		19	
20		20	
21		21	
22		22	
23		23	
24		24	
25		25	
26		26	
27		27	
28		28	
29		29	
30		30	
31			

JULY		AUGUST	
1		1	
2		2	
3		3	
4		4	
5		5	
6		6	
7		7	
8		8	
9		9	
10		10	
11		11	
12		12	
13		13	
14		14	
15		15	
16		16	
17		17	
18		18	
19		19	
20		20	
21		21	
22		22	
23		23	
24		24	
25		25	
26		26	
27		27	
28		28	
29		29	
30		30	
31		31	

SEPTEMBER		OCTOBER	
1		1	
2		2	
3		3	
4		4	
5		5	
6		6	
7		7	
8		8	
9		9	
10		10	
11		11	
12		12	
13		13	
14		14	
15		15	
16		16	
17		17	
18		18	
19		19	
20		20	
21		21	
22		22	
23		23	
24		24	
25		25	
26		26	
27		27	
28		28	
29		29	
30		30	
		31	

NOVEMBER		DECEMBER	
1		1	
2		2	
3		3	
4		4	
5		5	
6		6	
7		7	
8		8	
9		9	
10		10	
11		11	
12		12	
13		13	
14		14	
15		15	
16		16	
17		17	
18		18	
19		19	
20		20	
21		21	
22		22	
23		23	
24		24	
25		25	
26		26	
27		27	
28		28	
29		29	
30		30	
		31	

PRACTICE SESSION

DAY / DATE: _____ INSTRUMENT _____
Motivation: ☐ Low ☐ Medium ☐ High

TODAY'S FOCUS

1. _____
2. _____
3. _____

PRACTICE TIME

Planned: ☐ 10 ☐ 20 ☐ 30 ☐ 45 ☐ 60+ minutes   Actual Practice: _____

WHAT YOU PRACTICED TODAY

PLAYING: ☐ New Music ☐ Repertoire ☐ Excerpt Practice ☐ Riffs & Solos ☐ Improvisation
☐ Other: _____

TECHNIQUE & SKILLS: ☐ Scales ☐ Chords ☐ Arpeggios ☐ Ear Training ☐ Exercises
☐ Rhythm & Reading ☐ Applied Theory ☐ Other: _____

CREATIVITY: ☐ Songwriting ☐ Composition ☐ Improvisation ☐ Listening & Study ☐ Lyrics
☐ Other: _____

PERFORMANCE & PROJECTS: ☐ Recording ☐ Backing Tracks ☐ Group Work ☐ Research
☐ Other: _____

TEACHER / ASSIGNMENTS / IMPROVEMENTS

_____
_____
_____
_____
_____

PROGRESS SNAPSHOT (Circle how today's practice went:)

☹ 🙁 😐 🙂 😀

NEXT PRACTICE GOALS

_____
_____
_____

DAILY TIP:

Ultimately, your true love of music is what will keep you motivated to practice.

PRACTICE SESSION

DAY / DATE: _____ INSTRUMENT _____

Motivation: ☐ Low ☐ Medium ☐ High

TODAY'S FOCUS

1. _____
2. _____
3. _____

PRACTICE TIME

Planned: ☐ 10 ☐ 20 ☐ 30 ☐ 45 ☐ 60+ minutes   Actual Practice: _____

WHAT YOU PRACTICED TODAY

PLAYING: ☐ New Music ☐ Repertoire ☐ Excerpt Practice ☐ Riffs & Solos ☐ Improvisation
☐ Other: _____

TECHNIQUE & SKILLS: ☐ Scales ☐ Chords ☐ Arpeggios ☐ Ear Training ☐ Exercises
☐ Rhythm & Reading ☐ Applied Theory ☐ Other: _____

CREATIVITY: ☐ Songwriting ☐ Composition ☐ Improvisation ☐ Listening & Study ☐ Lyrics
☐ Other: _____

PERFORMANCE & PROJECTS: ☐ Recording ☐ Backing Tracks ☐ Group Work ☐ Research
☐ Other: _____

TEACHER / ASSIGNMENTS / IMPROVEMENTS

_____
_____
_____
_____
_____

PROGRESS SNAPSHOT (Circle how today's practice went:)

☹   😕   😐   🙂   😄

NEXT PRACTICE GOALS

_____
_____
_____
_____
_____

© 2025 Kalymi Music Publishing – brentrobitaille.com

PRACTICE SESSION
30

DAY / DATE: _____ INSTRUMENT _____
Motivation: ☐ Low ☐ Medium ☐ High

TODAY'S FOCUS
1. _____
2. _____
3. _____

PRACTICE TIME
Planned: ☐ 10 ☐ 20 ☐ 30 ☐ 45 ☐ 60+ minutes   Actual Practice: _____

WHAT YOU PRACTICED TODAY

PLAYING: ☐ New Music ☐ Repertoire ☐ Excerpt Practice ☐ Riffs & Solos ☐ Improvisation
☐ Other: _____

TECHNIQUE & SKILLS: ☐ Scales ☐ Chords ☐ Arpeggios ☐ Ear Training ☐ Exercises
☐ Rhythm & Reading ☐ Applied Theory ☐ Other: _____

CREATIVITY: ☐ Songwriting ☐ Composition ☐ Improvisation ☐ Listening & Study ☐ Lyrics
☐ Other: _____

PERFORMANCE & PROJECTS: ☐ Recording ☐ Backing Tracks ☐ Group Work ☐ Research
☐ Other: _____

TEACHER / ASSIGNMENTS / IMPROVEMENTS
_____
_____
_____
_____
_____

PROGRESS SNAPSHOT (Circle how today's practice went:)

☹ 🙁 😐 🙂 😃

NEXT PRACTICE GOALS
_____
_____
_____

DAILY TIP:
Amateurs practice until they get it right. Professionals practice until they can't get it wrong.

PRACTICE SESSION

DAY / DATE: _____ INSTRUMENT _____

Motivation: ☐ Low ☐ Medium ☐ High

TODAY'S FOCUS

1. _____
2. _____
3. _____

PRACTICE TIME

Planned: ☐ 10 ☐ 20 ☐ 30 ☐ 45 ☐ 60+ minutes   Actual Practice: _____

WHAT YOU PRACTICED TODAY

PLAYING: ☐ New Music ☐ Repertoire ☐ Excerpt Practice ☐ Riffs & Solos ☐ Improvisation
☐ Other: _____

TECHNIQUE & SKILLS: ☐ Scales ☐ Chords ☐ Arpeggios ☐ Ear Training ☐ Exercises
☐ Rhythm & Reading ☐ Applied Theory ☐ Other: _____

CREATIVITY: ☐ Songwriting ☐ Composition ☐ Improvisation ☐ Listening & Study ☐ Lyrics
☐ Other: _____

PERFORMANCE & PROJECTS: ☐ Recording ☐ Backing Tracks ☐ Group Work ☐ Research
☐ Other: _____

TEACHER / ASSIGNMENTS / IMPROVEMENTS

_____
_____
_____
_____
_____

PROGRESS SNAPSHOT (Circle how today's practice went:)

☹   🙁   😐   🙂   😀

NEXT PRACTICE GOALS

_____
_____
_____
_____
_____

DAY SESSION

PRACTICE SESSION

DAY / DATE: _____   INSTRUMENT _____

Motivation: ☐ Low   ☐ Medium   ☐ High

TODAY'S FOCUS

1. _____
2. _____
3. _____

PRACTICE TIME

Planned: ☐ 10   ☐ 20   ☐ 30   ☐ 45   ☐ 60+ minutes   Actual Practice: _____

WHAT YOU PRACTICED TODAY

PLAYING: ☐ New Music ☐ Repertoire ☐ Excerpt Practice ☐ Riffs & Solos ☐ Improvisation
☐ Other: _____

TECHNIQUE & SKILLS: ☐ Scales ☐ Chords ☐ Arpeggios ☐ Ear Training ☐ Exercises
☐ Rhythm & Reading ☐ Applied Theory ☐ Other: _____
_____

CREATIVITY: ☐ Songwriting ☐ Composition ☐ Improvisation ☐ Listening & Study ☐ Lyrics
☐ Other: _____

PERFORMANCE & PROJECTS: ☐ Recording ☐ Backing Tracks ☐ Group Work ☐ Research
☐ Other: _____

TEACHER / ASSIGNMENTS / IMPROVEMENTS

_____
_____
_____
_____
_____

PROGRESS SNAPSHOT (Circle how today's practice went:)

☹   🙁   😐   🙂   😄

NEXT PRACTICE GOALS

_____
_____
_____

DAILY TIP:

Practice is the best of all instructors. Publilius Syrus

PRACTICE SUMMARY

DATE RANGE: _____

TOTAL SESSIONS: _____ TOTAL TIME: _____

OVERALL FOCUS / ENERGY THIS PERIOD
☐ Strong Momentum ☐ Balanced Progress ☐ Slower Week ☐ Reset / Recovery

TOP 3 ACCOMPLISHMENTS
1. _____
2. _____
3. _____

WHAT YOU WORKED ON MOST

PLAYING: _____
_____

TECHNIQUE & SKILLS: _____
_____

CREATIVITY: _____
_____

PERFORMANCE & PROJECTS: _____
_____

DEEP PRACTICE RECAP
Piece / Exercise: _____
Current Metronome: _____ bpm   Goal: _____ bpm
Focus Area: ☐ Tone ☐ Timing ☐ Fingering ☐ Articulation ☐ Other
Improvement Plan: _____

PERFORMANCES
☐ Recorded / Video ☐ Played for Someone ☐ Ensemble / Jam ☐ None this Week

PROGRESS & INSIGHTS
What improved the most? _____
What still needs work? _____
Creative discoveries or ideas? _____

NEXT FOCUS / UPCOMING GOALS
_____
_____
_____

WEEKLY INSIGHT
If it feels easy, you are likely only practicing what you already know.

PRACTICE SESSION

DAY / DATE: _____ INSTRUMENT _____
Motivation: ☐ Low ☐ Medium ☐ High

TODAY'S FOCUS

1. _____
2. _____
3. _____

PRACTICE TIME

Planned: ☐ 10 ☐ 20 ☐ 30 ☐ 45 ☐ 60+ minutes   Actual Practice: _____

WHAT YOU PRACTICED TODAY

PLAYING: ☐ New Music ☐ Repertoire ☐ Excerpt Practice ☐ Riffs & Solos ☐ Improvisation
☐ Other: _____

TECHNIQUE & SKILLS: ☐ Scales ☐ Chords ☐ Arpeggios ☐ Ear Training ☐ Exercises
☐ Rhythm & Reading ☐ Applied Theory ☐ Other: _____

CREATIVITY: ☐ Songwriting ☐ Composition ☐ Improvisation ☐ Listening & Study ☐ Lyrics
☐ Other: _____

PERFORMANCE & PROJECTS: ☐ Recording ☐ Backing Tracks ☐ Group Work ☐ Research
☐ Other: _____

TEACHER / ASSIGNMENTS / IMPROVEMENTS

_____
_____
_____
_____
_____

PROGRESS SNAPSHOT (Circle how today's practice went:)

☹ 🙁 😐 🙂 😊

NEXT PRACTICE GOALS

_____
_____
_____

DAILY TIP:

It does not matter how slowly you go as long as you do not stop. Confucius

PRACTICE SESSION

DAY / DATE: _____ INSTRUMENT _____
Motivation: ☐ Low ☐ Medium ☐ High

TODAY'S FOCUS

1. _____
2. _____
3. _____

PRACTICE TIME

Planned: ☐ 10 ☐ 20 ☐ 30 ☐ 45 ☐ 60+ minutes   Actual Practice: _____

WHAT YOU PRACTICED TODAY

PLAYING: ☐ New Music ☐ Repertoire ☐ Excerpt Practice ☐ Riffs & Solos ☐ Improvisation
☐ Other: _____

TECHNIQUE & SKILLS: ☐ Scales ☐ Chords ☐ Arpeggios ☐ Ear Training ☐ Exercises
☐ Rhythm & Reading ☐ Applied Theory ☐ Other: _____

CREATIVITY: ☐ Songwriting ☐ Composition ☐ Improvisation ☐ Listening & Study ☐ Lyrics
☐ Other: _____

PERFORMANCE & PROJECTS: ☐ Recording ☐ Backing Tracks ☐ Group Work ☐ Research
☐ Other: _____

TEACHER / ASSIGNMENTS / IMPROVEMENTS

_____
_____
_____
_____
_____

PROGRESS SNAPSHOT (Circle how today's practice went:)

😠   ☹️   😐   🙂   😄

NEXT PRACTICE GOALS

_____
_____
_____
_____
_____

DAY SESSION

PRACTICE SESSION

DAY / DATE: _____ INSTRUMENT _____
Motivation: ☐ Low ☐ Medium ☐ High

TODAY'S FOCUS

1. _____
2. _____
3. _____

PRACTICE TIME

Planned: ☐ 10 ☐ 20 ☐ 30 ☐ 45 ☐ 60+ minutes   Actual Practice: _____

WHAT YOU PRACTICED TODAY

PLAYING: ☐ New Music ☐ Repertoire ☐ Excerpt Practice ☐ Riffs & Solos ☐ Improvisation
☐ Other: _____

TECHNIQUE & SKILLS: ☐ Scales ☐ Chords ☐ Arpeggios ☐ Ear Training ☐ Exercises
☐ Rhythm & Reading ☐ Applied Theory ☐ Other: _____
_____

CREATIVITY: ☐ Songwriting ☐ Composition ☐ Improvisation ☐ Listening & Study ☐ Lyrics
☐ Other: _____

PERFORMANCE & PROJECTS: ☐ Recording ☐ Backing Tracks ☐ Group Work ☐ Research
☐ Other: _____

TEACHER / ASSIGNMENTS / IMPROVEMENTS

_____
_____
_____
_____
_____

PROGRESS SNAPSHOT (Circle how today's practice went:)

😠   ☹️   😐   🙂   😄

NEXT PRACTICE GOALS

_____
_____
_____

DAILY TIP:

Notice where the tension is in your body before playing a single note.

PRACTICE SESSION

DAY / DATE: _____ INSTRUMENT _____
Motivation: ☐ Low   ☐ Medium   ☐ High

TODAY'S FOCUS
1. _____
2. _____
3. _____

PRACTICE TIME
Planned: ☐ 10 ☐ 20 ☐ 30 ☐ 45 ☐ 60+ minutes   Actual Practice: _____

WHAT YOU PRACTICED TODAY

PLAYING: ☐ New Music   ☐ Repertoire   ☐ Excerpt Practice   ☐ Riffs & Solos   ☐ Improvisation
☐ Other: _____

TECHNIQUE & SKILLS: ☐ Scales   ☐ Chords   ☐ Arpeggios   ☐ Ear Training   ☐ Exercises
☐ Rhythm & Reading   ☐ Applied Theory   ☐ Other: _____

CREATIVITY: ☐ Songwriting   ☐ Composition   ☐ Improvisation   ☐ Listening & Study   ☐ Lyrics
☐ Other: _____

PERFORMANCE & PROJECTS: ☐ Recording   ☐ Backing Tracks   ☐ Group Work   ☐ Research
☐ Other: _____

TEACHER / ASSIGNMENTS / IMPROVEMENTS
_____
_____
_____
_____
_____

PROGRESS SNAPSHOT (Circle how today's practice went:)

😠   ☹️   😐   🙂   😄

NEXT PRACTICE GOALS
_____
_____
_____
_____
_____

DAY SESSION

PRACTICE SESSION

DAY / DATE: _____ INSTRUMENT _____
Motivation: ☐ Low ☐ Medium ☐ High

TODAY'S FOCUS
1. _____
2. _____
3. _____

PRACTICE TIME
Planned: ☐ 10 ☐ 20 ☐ 30 ☐ 45 ☐ 60+ minutes   Actual Practice: _____

WHAT YOU PRACTICED TODAY

PLAYING: ☐ New Music ☐ Repertoire ☐ Excerpt Practice ☐ Riffs & Solos ☐ Improvisation
☐ Other: _____

TECHNIQUE & SKILLS: ☐ Scales ☐ Chords ☐ Arpeggios ☐ Ear Training ☐ Exercises
☐ Rhythm & Reading ☐ Applied Theory ☐ Other: _____

CREATIVITY: ☐ Songwriting ☐ Composition ☐ Improvisation ☐ Listening & Study ☐ Lyrics
☐ Other: _____

PERFORMANCE & PROJECTS: ☐ Recording ☐ Backing Tracks ☐ Group Work ☐ Research
☐ Other: _____

TEACHER / ASSIGNMENTS / IMPROVEMENTS
_____
_____
_____
_____
_____

PROGRESS SNAPSHOT (Circle how today's practice went:)

😠 🙁 😐 🙂 😄

NEXT PRACTICE GOALS
_____
_____
_____

DAILY TIP:
Write the word "breathe" on sticky paper to keep focused.

PRACTICE SUMMARY

DATE RANGE: _____

TOTAL SESSIONS: _____ TOTAL TIME: _____

OVERALL FOCUS / ENERGY THIS PERIOD
☐ Strong Momentum ☐ Balanced Progress ☐ Slower Week ☐ Reset / Recovery

TOP 3 ACCOMPLISHMENTS
1. _____
2. _____
3. _____

WHAT YOU WORKED ON MOST
PLAYING: _____
_____

TECHNIQUE & SKILLS: _____
_____

CREATIVITY: _____
_____

PERFORMANCE & PROJECTS: _____
_____

DEEP PRACTICE RECAP
Piece / Exercise: _____
Current Metronome: _____ bpm   Goal: _____ bpm
Focus Area: ☐ Tone ☐ Timing ☐ Fingering ☐ Articulation ☐ Other
Improvement Plan: _____

PERFORMANCES
☐ Recorded / Video ☐ Played for Someone ☐ Ensemble /Jam ☐ None this Week

PROGRESS & INSIGHTS
What improved the most? _____
What still needs work? _____
Creative discoveries or ideas? _____

NEXT FOCUS / UPCOMING GOALS
_____
_____
_____

WEEKLY INSIGHT
What is best in music is not to be found in the notes. Gustav Mahler

TEACHER / LESSON NOTES

LESSON DATE: _____ INSTRUMENT _____
Readiness: ☐ Low ☐ Medium ☐ High

ASSIGNMENTS / FOCUS POINTS

1. _____
2. _____
3. _____
4. _____
5. _____

HOW LONG YOU SHOULD PRACTICE AT EACH SESSION

Planned: ☐ 10 ☐ 20 ☐ 30 ☐ 45 ☐ 60+ minutes   Other: _____

TECHNIQUE & SKILLS: ☐ Scales ☐ Chords ☐ Arpeggios ☐ Ear Training ☐ Exercises
☐ Rhythm & Reading ☐ Applied Theory ☐ Other: _____
_____
_____

REPERTOIRE 1
Title / Section: _____
Measures / Focus: _____ Tempo Goal: _____ bpm

REPERTOIRE 2
Title / Section: _____
Measures / Focus: _____ Tempo Goal: _____ bpm

REPERTOIRE 3
Title / Section: _____
Measures / Focus: _____ Tempo Goal: _____ bpm

TEACHER COMMENTS
_____
_____
_____
_____
_____

STUDENT NOTES
_____
_____
_____

IDEAS & NOTES

PRACTICE SESSION

DAY / DATE: _____ INSTRUMENT _____
Motivation: ☐ Low ☐ Medium ☐ High

TODAY'S FOCUS

1. _____
2. _____
3. _____

PRACTICE TIME

Planned: ☐ 10 ☐ 20 ☐ 30 ☐ 45 ☐ 60+ minutes   Actual Practice: _____

WHAT YOU PRACTICED TODAY

PLAYING: ☐ New Music ☐ Repertoire ☐ Excerpt Practice ☐ Riffs & Solos ☐ Improvisation
☐ Other: _____

TECHNIQUE & SKILLS: ☐ Scales ☐ Chords ☐ Arpeggios ☐ Ear Training ☐ Exercises
☐ Rhythm & Reading ☐ Applied Theory ☐ Other: _____

_____

CREATIVITY: ☐ Songwriting ☐ Composition ☐ Improvisation ☐ Listening & Study ☐ Lyrics
☐ Other: _____

PERFORMANCE & PROJECTS: ☐ Recording ☐ Backing Tracks ☐ Group Work ☐ Research
☐ Other: _____

TEACHER / ASSIGNMENTS / IMPROVEMENTS

_____
_____
_____
_____
_____

PROGRESS SNAPSHOT (Circle how today's practice went:)

☹ 🙁 😐 🙂 😃

NEXT PRACTICE GOALS

_____
_____
_____

DAILY TIP:

Remember that learning an instrument is a marathon, not a sprint; pace yourself for the long run.

PRACTICE SESSION

DAY / DATE: _____ INSTRUMENT _____
Motivation: ☐ Low ☐ Medium ☐ High

TODAY'S FOCUS

1. _____
2. _____
3. _____

PRACTICE TIME

Planned: ☐ 10 ☐ 20 ☐ 30 ☐ 45 ☐ 60+ minutes   Actual Practice: _____

WHAT YOU PRACTICED TODAY

PLAYING: ☐ New Music ☐ Repertoire ☐ Excerpt Practice ☐ Riffs & Solos ☐ Improvisation
☐ Other: _____

TECHNIQUE & SKILLS: ☐ Scales ☐ Chords ☐ Arpeggios ☐ Ear Training ☐ Exercises
☐ Rhythm & Reading ☐ Applied Theory ☐ Other: _____

CREATIVITY: ☐ Songwriting ☐ Composition ☐ Improvisation ☐ Listening & Study ☐ Lyrics
☐ Other: _____

PERFORMANCE & PROJECTS: ☐ Recording ☐ Backing Tracks ☐ Group Work ☐ Research
☐ Other: _____

TEACHER / ASSIGNMENTS / IMPROVEMENTS

_____
_____
_____
_____
_____

PROGRESS SNAPSHOT (Circle how today's practice went:)

☹ 🙁 😐 🙂 😄

NEXT PRACTICE GOALS

_____
_____
_____
_____
_____

DAY SESSION

PRACTICE SESSION

DAY / DATE: _____ INSTRUMENT _____
Motivation: ☐ Low ☐ Medium ☐ High

TODAY'S FOCUS

1. _____
2. _____
3. _____

PRACTICE TIME

Planned: ☐ 10 ☐ 20 ☐ 30 ☐ 45 ☐ 60+ minutes   Actual Practice: _____

WHAT YOU PRACTICED TODAY

PLAYING: ☐ New Music ☐ Repertoire ☐ Excerpt Practice ☐ Riffs & Solos ☐ Improvisation
☐ Other: _____

TECHNIQUE & SKILLS: ☐ Scales ☐ Chords ☐ Arpeggios ☐ Ear Training ☐ Exercises
☐ Rhythm & Reading ☐ Applied Theory ☐ Other: _____

CREATIVITY: ☐ Songwriting ☐ Composition ☐ Improvisation ☐ Listening & Study ☐ Lyrics
☐ Other: _____

PERFORMANCE & PROJECTS: ☐ Recording ☐ Backing Tracks ☐ Group Work ☐ Research
☐ Other: _____

TEACHER / ASSIGNMENTS / IMPROVEMENTS

_____
_____
_____
_____
_____

PROGRESS SNAPSHOT (Circle how today's practice went:)

☹ 🙁 😐 🙂 😄

NEXT PRACTICE GOALS

_____
_____
_____

DAILY TIP:

Schedule a small performance each week, no matter how small (even if it's for your cat!).

PRACTICE SESSION

DAY / DATE: _____ INSTRUMENT _____
Motivation: ☐ Low ☐ Medium ☐ High

TODAY'S FOCUS
1. _____
2. _____
3. _____

PRACTICE TIME
Planned: ☐ 10 ☐ 20 ☐ 30 ☐ 45 ☐ 60+ minutes   Actual Practice: _____

WHAT YOU PRACTICED TODAY

PLAYING: ☐ New Music ☐ Repertoire ☐ Excerpt Practice ☐ Riffs & Solos ☐ Improvisation
☐ Other: _____

TECHNIQUE & SKILLS: ☐ Scales ☐ Chords ☐ Arpeggios ☐ Ear Training ☐ Exercises
☐ Rhythm & Reading ☐ Applied Theory ☐ Other: _____

CREATIVITY: ☐ Songwriting ☐ Composition ☐ Improvisation ☐ Listening & Study ☐ Lyrics
☐ Other: _____

PERFORMANCE & PROJECTS: ☐ Recording ☐ Backing Tracks ☐ Group Work ☐ Research
☐ Other: _____

TEACHER / ASSIGNMENTS / IMPROVEMENTS
_____
_____
_____
_____
_____

PROGRESS SNAPSHOT (Circle how today's practice went:)

😠   ☹   😐   🙂   😀

NEXT PRACTICE GOALS
_____
_____
_____
_____
_____

DAY SESSION

PRACTICE SESSION

DAY / DATE: _____ INSTRUMENT _____
Motivation: ☐ Low   ☐ Medium   ☐ High

TODAY'S FOCUS

1. _____
2. _____
3. _____

PRACTICE TIME

Planned: ☐ 10 ☐ 20 ☐ 30 ☐ 45 ☐ 60+ minutes   Actual Practice: _____

WHAT YOU PRACTICED TODAY

PLAYING: ☐ New Music ☐ Repertoire ☐ Excerpt Practice ☐ Riffs & Solos ☐ Improvisation
☐ Other: _____

TECHNIQUE & SKILLS: ☐ Scales ☐ Chords ☐ Arpeggios ☐ Ear Training ☐ Exercises
☐ Rhythm & Reading ☐ Applied Theory ☐ Other: _____

CREATIVITY: ☐ Songwriting ☐ Composition ☐ Improvisation ☐ Listening & Study ☐ Lyrics
☐ Other: _____

PERFORMANCE & PROJECTS: ☐ Recording ☐ Backing Tracks ☐ Group Work ☐ Research
☐ Other: _____

TEACHER / ASSIGNMENTS / IMPROVEMENTS

_____
_____
_____
_____
_____

PROGRESS SNAPSHOT (Circle how today's practice went:)

☹   🙁   😐   🙂   😄

NEXT PRACTICE GOALS

_____
_____
_____

DAILY TIP:

Before a performance, make sure you can play your piece 90 percent correctly 100 percent of the time. The extra 10% is artistic license.

PRACTICE SUMMARY

DATE RANGE: _____
TOTAL SESSIONS: _____ TOTAL TIME: _____

OVERALL FOCUS / ENERGY THIS PERIOD
☐ Strong Momentum ☐ Balanced Progress ☐ Slower Week ☐ Reset / Recovery

TOP 3 ACCOMPLISHMENTS
1. _____
2. _____
3. _____

WHAT YOU WORKED ON MOST
PLAYING: _____
_____

TECHNIQUE & SKILLS: _____
_____

CREATIVITY: _____
_____

PERFORMANCE & PROJECTS: _____
_____

DEEP PRACTICE RECAP
Piece / Exercise: _____
Current Metronome: _____ bpm   Goal: _____ bpm
Focus Area: ☐ Tone ☐ Timing ☐ Fingering ☐ Articulation ☐ Other
Improvement Plan: _____

PERFORMANCES
☐ Recorded / Video ☐ Played for Someone ☐ Ensemble /Jam ☐ None this Week

PROGRESS & INSIGHTS
What improved the most? _____
What still needs work? _____
Creative discoveries or ideas? _____

NEXT FOCUS / UPCOMING GOALS
_____
_____
_____

WEEKLY INSIGHT
Music begins where the possibilities of language end. Jean Sibelius

PRACTICE SESSION

DAY / DATE: _____ INSTRUMENT _____

Motivation: ☐ Low   ☐ Medium   ☐ High

TODAY'S FOCUS

1. _____
2. _____
3. _____

PRACTICE TIME

Planned: ☐ 10 ☐ 20 ☐ 30 ☐ 45 ☐ 60+ minutes   Actual Practice: _____

WHAT YOU PRACTICED TODAY

PLAYING: ☐ New Music ☐ Repertoire ☐ Excerpt Practice ☐ Riffs & Solos ☐ Improvisation
☐ Other: _____

TECHNIQUE & SKILLS: ☐ Scales ☐ Chords ☐ Arpeggios ☐ Ear Training ☐ Exercises
☐ Rhythm & Reading ☐ Applied Theory ☐ Other: _____

CREATIVITY: ☐ Songwriting ☐ Composition ☐ Improvisation ☐ Listening & Study ☐ Lyrics
☐ Other: _____

PERFORMANCE & PROJECTS: ☐ Recording ☐ Backing Tracks ☐ Group Work ☐ Research
☐ Other: _____

TEACHER / ASSIGNMENTS / IMPROVEMENTS

_____
_____
_____
_____
_____

PROGRESS SNAPSHOT (Circle how today's practice went:)

☹   🙁   😐   🙂   😃

NEXT PRACTICE GOALS

_____
_____
_____

DAILY TIP:

Mentally practice fingerings away from your instrument to strengthen memory.

PRACTICE SESSION

DAY / DATE: _____ INSTRUMENT _____
Motivation: ☐ Low ☐ Medium ☐ High

TODAY'S FOCUS
1. _____
2. _____
3. _____

PRACTICE TIME
Planned: ☐ 10 ☐ 20 ☐ 30 ☐ 45 ☐ 60+ minutes   Actual Practice: _____

WHAT YOU PRACTICED TODAY

PLAYING: ☐ New Music ☐ Repertoire ☐ Excerpt Practice ☐ Riffs & Solos ☐ Improvisation
☐ Other: _____

TECHNIQUE & SKILLS: ☐ Scales ☐ Chords ☐ Arpeggios ☐ Ear Training ☐ Exercises
☐ Rhythm & Reading ☐ Applied Theory ☐ Other: _____

CREATIVITY: ☐ Songwriting ☐ Composition ☐ Improvisation ☐ Listening & Study ☐ Lyrics
☐ Other: _____

PERFORMANCE & PROJECTS: ☐ Recording ☐ Backing Tracks ☐ Group Work ☐ Research
☐ Other: _____

TEACHER / ASSIGNMENTS / IMPROVEMENTS
_____
_____
_____
_____
_____

PROGRESS SNAPSHOT (Circle how today's practice went:)

☹ 🙁 😐 🙂 😊

NEXT PRACTICE GOALS
_____
_____
_____
_____
_____

DAY SESSION

PRACTICE SESSION
50

DAY / DATE: _____ INSTRUMENT _____

Motivation: ☐ Low ☐ Medium ☐ High

TODAY'S FOCUS

1. _____
2. _____
3. _____

PRACTICE TIME

Planned: ☐ 10 ☐ 20 ☐ 30 ☐ 45 ☐ 60+ minutes   Actual Practice: _____

WHAT YOU PRACTICED TODAY

PLAYING: ☐ New Music ☐ Repertoire ☐ Excerpt Practice ☐ Riffs & Solos ☐ Improvisation
☐ Other: _____

TECHNIQUE & SKILLS: ☐ Scales ☐ Chords ☐ Arpeggios ☐ Ear Training ☐ Exercises
☐ Rhythm & Reading ☐ Applied Theory ☐ Other: _____

CREATIVITY: ☐ Songwriting ☐ Composition ☐ Improvisation ☐ Listening & Study ☐ Lyrics
☐ Other: _____

PERFORMANCE & PROJECTS: ☐ Recording ☐ Backing Tracks ☐ Group Work ☐ Research
☐ Other: _____

TEACHER / ASSIGNMENTS / IMPROVEMENTS

_____
_____
_____
_____
_____

PROGRESS SNAPSHOT (Circle how today's practice went:)

☹ 🙁 😐 🙂 😄

NEXT PRACTICE GOALS

_____
_____
_____

DAILY TIP:

Record or video yourself often and listen as a listener.

PRACTICE SESSION

DAY / DATE: _____ INSTRUMENT _____

Motivation: ☐ Low ☐ Medium ☐ High

TODAY'S FOCUS

1. _____
2. _____
3. _____

PRACTICE TIME

Planned: ☐ 10 ☐ 20 ☐ 30 ☐ 45 ☐ 60+ minutes   Actual Practice: _____

WHAT YOU PRACTICED TODAY

PLAYING: ☐ New Music ☐ Repertoire ☐ Excerpt Practice ☐ Riffs & Solos ☐ Improvisation
☐ Other: _____

TECHNIQUE & SKILLS: ☐ Scales ☐ Chords ☐ Arpeggios ☐ Ear Training ☐ Exercises
☐ Rhythm & Reading ☐ Applied Theory ☐ Other: _____

CREATIVITY: ☐ Songwriting ☐ Composition ☐ Improvisation ☐ Listening & Study ☐ Lyrics
☐ Other: _____

PERFORMANCE & PROJECTS: ☐ Recording ☐ Backing Tracks ☐ Group Work ☐ Research
☐ Other: _____

TEACHER / ASSIGNMENTS / IMPROVEMENTS

_____
_____
_____
_____
_____

PROGRESS SNAPSHOT (Circle how today's practice went:)

☹ 🙁 😐 🙂 😄

NEXT PRACTICE GOALS

_____
_____
_____
_____
_____

PRACTICE SESSION

DAY / DATE: _____ INSTRUMENT _____

Motivation: ☐ Low   ☐ Medium   ☐ High

TODAY'S FOCUS

1. _____
2. _____
3. _____

PRACTICE TIME

Planned: ☐ 10 ☐ 20 ☐ 30 ☐ 45 ☐ 60+ minutes   Actual Practice: _____

WHAT YOU PRACTICED TODAY

PLAYING: ☐ New Music ☐ Repertoire ☐ Excerpt Practice ☐ Riffs & Solos ☐ Improvisation
☐ Other: _____

TECHNIQUE & SKILLS: ☐ Scales ☐ Chords ☐ Arpeggios ☐ Ear Training ☐ Exercises
☐ Rhythm & Reading ☐ Applied Theory ☐ Other: _____

CREATIVITY: ☐ Songwriting ☐ Composition ☐ Improvisation ☐ Listening & Study ☐ Lyrics
☐ Other: _____

PERFORMANCE & PROJECTS: ☐ Recording ☐ Backing Tracks ☐ Group Work ☐ Research
☐ Other: _____

TEACHER / ASSIGNMENTS / IMPROVEMENTS

_____
_____
_____
_____
_____

PROGRESS SNAPSHOT (Circle how today's practice went:)

☹ 🙁 😐 🙂 😄

NEXT PRACTICE GOALS

_____
_____
_____

DAILY TIP:

Lock in your rhythm by practicing with backing tracks or other musicians.

PRACTICE SUMMARY

DATE RANGE: _____
TOTAL SESSIONS: _____ TOTAL TIME: _____

OVERALL FOCUS / ENERGY THIS PERIOD
☐ Strong Momentum ☐ Balanced Progress ☐ Slower Week ☐ Reset / Recovery

TOP 3 ACCOMPLISHMENTS
1. _____
2. _____
3. _____

WHAT YOU WORKED ON MOST
PLAYING: _____
_____

TECHNIQUE & SKILLS: _____
_____

CREATIVITY: _____
_____

PERFORMANCE & PROJECTS: _____
_____

DEEP PRACTICE RECAP
Piece / Exercise: _____
Current Metronome: _____ bpm   Goal: _____ bpm
Focus Area: ☐ Tone ☐ Timing ☐ Fingering ☐ Articulation ☐ Other
Improvement Plan: _____

PERFORMANCES
☐ Recorded / Video ☐ Played for Someone ☐ Ensemble / Jam ☐ None this Week

PROGRESS & INSIGHTS
What improved the most? _____
What still needs work? _____
Creative discoveries or ideas? _____

NEXT FOCUS / UPCOMING GOALS
_____
_____
_____

WEEKLY INSIGHT
A good composer does not imitate; he steals. Igor Stravinsky

TEACHER / LESSON NOTES

LESSON DATE: _____ INSTRUMENT _____

Readiness: ☐ Low ☐ Medium ☐ High

ASSIGNMENTS / FOCUS POINTS

1. _____
2. _____
3. _____
4. _____
5. _____

HOW LONG YOU SHOULD PRACTICE AT EACH SESSION

Planned: ☐ 10 ☐ 20 ☐ 30 ☐ 45 ☐ 60+ minutes   Other: _____

TECHNIQUE & SKILLS: ☐ Scales ☐ Chords ☐ Arpeggios ☐ Ear Training ☐ Exercises
☐ Rhythm & Reading ☐ Applied Theory ☐ Other: _____
_____
_____

REPERTOIRE 1
Title / Section: _____
Measures / Focus: _____ Tempo Goal: _____ bpm

REPERTOIRE 2
Title / Section: _____
Measures / Focus: _____ Tempo Goal: _____ bpm

REPERTOIRE 3
Title / Section: _____
Measures / Focus: _____ Tempo Goal: _____ bpm

TEACHER COMMENTS
_____
_____
_____
_____
_____

STUDENT NOTES
_____
_____
_____

IDEAS & NOTES

MONTHLY REFLECTION

MONTH: _____ TOTAL TIME: _____
TOTAL SESSIONS: _____ TOTAL PERFORMANCES: _____

RATE YOUR PROGRESS THIS MONTH: BELOW ★   AVERAGE ★ ★   ABOVE ★ ★ ★

WHAT ARE YOU MOST GRATEFUL FOR WITH YOUR MUSIC THIS MONTH

_____
_____
_____
_____
_____

SET YOUR GOALS FOR NEXT MONTH

_____
_____
_____
_____
_____

POSITIVE LESSONS OR HABITS TO CONTINUE NEXT MONTH

_____
_____
_____
_____
_____

NOTES

_____
_____
_____
_____
_____

INSIGHT

Practice slowly; then even slower. – Franz Liszt

Creative blocks usually mean one thing: you've starting from the wrong point.

PRACTICE SESSION

DAY / DATE: _____ INSTRUMENT _____

Motivation: ☐ Low ☐ Medium ☐ High

TODAY'S FOCUS

1. _____
2. _____
3. _____

PRACTICE TIME

Planned: ☐ 10 ☐ 20 ☐ 30 ☐ 45 ☐ 60+ minutes   Actual Practice: _____

WHAT YOU PRACTICED TODAY

PLAYING: ☐ New Music ☐ Repertoire ☐ Excerpt Practice ☐ Riffs & Solos ☐ Improvisation
☐ Other: _____

TECHNIQUE & SKILLS: ☐ Scales ☐ Chords ☐ Arpeggios ☐ Ear Training ☐ Exercises
☐ Rhythm & Reading ☐ Applied Theory ☐ Other: _____

CREATIVITY: ☐ Songwriting ☐ Composition ☐ Improvisation ☐ Listening & Study ☐ Lyrics
☐ Other: _____

PERFORMANCE & PROJECTS: ☐ Recording ☐ Backing Tracks ☐ Group Work ☐ Research
☐ Other: _____

TEACHER / ASSIGNMENTS / IMPROVEMENTS

_____
_____
_____
_____
_____

PROGRESS SNAPSHOT (Circle how today's practice went:)

☹ 🙁 😐 🙂 😄

NEXT PRACTICE GOALS

_____
_____
_____

DAILY TIP:

Use elaboration to connect new material to existing knowledge for deeper comprehension.

PRACTICE SESSION

DAY / DATE: _____ INSTRUMENT _____
Motivation: ☐ Low ☐ Medium ☐ High

TODAY'S FOCUS
1. _____
2. _____
3. _____

PRACTICE TIME
Planned: ☐ 10 ☐ 20 ☐ 30 ☐ 45 ☐ 60+ minutes   Actual Practice: _____

WHAT YOU PRACTICED TODAY

PLAYING: ☐ New Music ☐ Repertoire ☐ Excerpt Practice ☐ Riffs & Solos ☐ Improvisation
☐ Other: _____

TECHNIQUE & SKILLS: ☐ Scales ☐ Chords ☐ Arpeggios ☐ Ear Training ☐ Exercises
☐ Rhythm & Reading ☐ Applied Theory ☐ Other: _____
_____

CREATIVITY: ☐ Songwriting ☐ Composition ☐ Improvisation ☐ Listening & Study ☐ Lyrics
☐ Other: _____

PERFORMANCE & PROJECTS: ☐ Recording ☐ Backing Tracks ☐ Group Work ☐ Research
☐ Other: _____

TEACHER / ASSIGNMENTS / IMPROVEMENTS
_____
_____
_____
_____
_____

PROGRESS SNAPSHOT (Circle how today's practice went:)
☹ 🙁 😐 🙂 😊

NEXT PRACTICE GOALS
_____
_____
_____
_____
_____

DAY SESSION

PRACTICE SESSION

DAY / DATE: _____   INSTRUMENT _____
Motivation: ☐ Low   ☐ Medium   ☐ High

TODAY'S FOCUS

1. _____
2. _____
3. _____

PRACTICE TIME

Planned: ☐ 10   ☐ 20   ☐ 30   ☐ 45   ☐ 60+ minutes   Actual Practice: _____

WHAT YOU PRACTICED TODAY

PLAYING: ☐ New Music ☐ Repertoire ☐ Excerpt Practice ☐ Riffs & Solos ☐ Improvisation
☐ Other: _____

TECHNIQUE & SKILLS: ☐ Scales ☐ Chords ☐ Arpeggios ☐ Ear Training ☐ Exercises
☐ Rhythm & Reading ☐ Applied Theory ☐ Other: _____

CREATIVITY: ☐ Songwriting ☐ Composition ☐ Improvisation ☐ Listening & Study ☐ Lyrics
☐ Other: _____

PERFORMANCE & PROJECTS: ☐ Recording ☐ Backing Tracks ☐ Group Work ☐ Research
☐ Other: _____

TEACHER / ASSIGNMENTS / IMPROVEMENTS

_____
_____
_____
_____
_____

PROGRESS SNAPSHOT (Circle how today's practice went:)

☹   🙁   😐   🙂   😃

NEXT PRACTICE GOALS

_____
_____
_____

DAILY TIP:

Use spaced repetition by increasing the time you practice specific pieces to move skills into long-term memory.

PRACTICE SESSION

DAY / DATE: _____ INSTRUMENT _____
Motivation: ☐ Low ☐ Medium ☐ High

TODAY'S FOCUS
1. _____
2. _____
3. _____

PRACTICE TIME
Planned: ☐ 10 ☐ 20 ☐ 30 ☐ 45 ☐ 60+ minutes   Actual Practice: _____

WHAT YOU PRACTICED TODAY

PLAYING: ☐ New Music ☐ Repertoire ☐ Excerpt Practice ☐ Riffs & Solos ☐ Improvisation
☐ Other: _____

TECHNIQUE & SKILLS: ☐ Scales ☐ Chords ☐ Arpeggios ☐ Ear Training ☐ Exercises
☐ Rhythm & Reading ☐ Applied Theory ☐ Other: _____

CREATIVITY: ☐ Songwriting ☐ Composition ☐ Improvisation ☐ Listening & Study ☐ Lyrics
☐ Other: _____

PERFORMANCE & PROJECTS: ☐ Recording ☐ Backing Tracks ☐ Group Work ☐ Research
☐ Other: _____

TEACHER / ASSIGNMENTS / IMPROVEMENTS
_____
_____
_____
_____
_____

PROGRESS SNAPSHOT (Circle how today's practice went:)

☹ 🙁 😐 🙂 😊

NEXT PRACTICE GOALS
_____
_____
_____
_____
_____

DAY SESSION

PRACTICE SESSION

DAY / DATE: _____   INSTRUMENT _____

Motivation: ☐ Low   ☐ Medium   ☐ High

TODAY'S FOCUS

1. _____
2. _____
3. _____

PRACTICE TIME

Planned: ☐ 10 ☐ 20 ☐ 30 ☐ 45 ☐ 60+ minutes   Actual Practice: _____

WHAT YOU PRACTICED TODAY

PLAYING: ☐ New Music ☐ Repertoire ☐ Excerpt Practice ☐ Riffs & Solos ☐ Improvisation
☐ Other: _____

TECHNIQUE & SKILLS: ☐ Scales ☐ Chords ☐ Arpeggios ☐ Ear Training ☐ Exercises
☐ Rhythm & Reading ☐ Applied Theory ☐ Other: _____

CREATIVITY: ☐ Songwriting ☐ Composition ☐ Improvisation ☐ Listening & Study ☐ Lyrics
☐ Other: _____

PERFORMANCE & PROJECTS: ☐ Recording ☐ Backing Tracks ☐ Group Work ☐ Research
☐ Other: _____

TEACHER / ASSIGNMENTS / IMPROVEMENTS

_____
_____
_____
_____
_____
_____

PROGRESS SNAPSHOT (Circle how today's practice went:)

☹   😕   😐   🙂   😄

NEXT PRACTICE GOALS

_____
_____
_____

DAILY TIP:

Treat practice as a non-negotiable habit and a consistent part of your daily routine.

PRACTICE SUMMARY

DATE RANGE: _____

TOTAL SESSIONS: _____ TOTAL TIME: _____

OVERALL FOCUS / ENERGY THIS PERIOD
☐ Strong Momentum ☐ Balanced Progress ☐ Slower Week ☐ Reset / Recovery

TOP 3 ACCOMPLISHMENTS
1. _____
2. _____
3. _____

WHAT YOU WORKED ON MOST

PLAYING: _____

TECHNIQUE & SKILLS: _____

CREATIVITY: _____

PERFORMANCE & PROJECTS: _____

DEEP PRACTICE RECAP
Piece / Exercise: _____
Current Metronome: _____ bpm   Goal: _____ bpm
Focus Area: ☐ Tone ☐ Timing ☐ Fingering ☐ Articulation ☐ Other
Improvement Plan: _____

PERFORMANCES
☐ Recorded / Video ☐ Played for Someone ☐ Ensemble / Jam ☐ None this Week

PROGRESS & INSIGHTS
What improved the most? _____
What still needs work? _____
Creative discoveries or ideas? _____

NEXT FOCUS / UPCOMING GOALS
_____
_____
_____

WEEKLY INSIGHT

Only from the heart can you touch the sky. Rumi

PRACTICE SESSION

DAY / DATE: _____ INSTRUMENT _____
Motivation: ☐ Low ☐ Medium ☐ High

TODAY'S FOCUS

1. _____
2. _____
3. _____

PRACTICE TIME

Planned: ☐ 10 ☐ 20 ☐ 30 ☐ 45 ☐ 60+ minutes   Actual Practice: _____

WHAT YOU PRACTICED TODAY

PLAYING: ☐ New Music ☐ Repertoire ☐ Excerpt Practice ☐ Riffs & Solos ☐ Improvisation
☐ Other: _____

TECHNIQUE & SKILLS: ☐ Scales ☐ Chords ☐ Arpeggios ☐ Ear Training ☐ Exercises
☐ Rhythm & Reading ☐ Applied Theory ☐ Other: _____

CREATIVITY: ☐ Songwriting ☐ Composition ☐ Improvisation ☐ Listening & Study ☐ Lyrics
☐ Other: _____

PERFORMANCE & PROJECTS: ☐ Recording ☐ Backing Tracks ☐ Group Work ☐ Research
☐ Other: _____

TEACHER / ASSIGNMENTS / IMPROVEMENTS

_____
_____
_____
_____
_____

PROGRESS SNAPSHOT (Circle how today's practice went:)

☹ 🙁 😐 🙂 😃

NEXT PRACTICE GOALS

_____
_____
_____

DAILY TIP:

Take regular breaks during long sessions to allow synapses to connect.

PRACTICE SESSION

DAY / DATE: _____ INSTRUMENT _____

Motivation: ☐ Low ☐ Medium ☐ High

TODAY'S FOCUS

1. _____
2. _____
3. _____

PRACTICE TIME

Planned: ☐ 10 ☐ 20 ☐ 30 ☐ 45 ☐ 60+ minutes   Actual Practice: _____

WHAT YOU PRACTICED TODAY

PLAYING: ☐ New Music ☐ Repertoire ☐ Excerpt Practice ☐ Riffs & Solos ☐ Improvisation
☐ Other: _____

TECHNIQUE & SKILLS: ☐ Scales ☐ Chords ☐ Arpeggios ☐ Ear Training ☐ Exercises
☐ Rhythm & Reading ☐ Applied Theory ☐ Other: _____

CREATIVITY: ☐ Songwriting ☐ Composition ☐ Improvisation ☐ Listening & Study ☐ Lyrics
☐ Other: _____

PERFORMANCE & PROJECTS: ☐ Recording ☐ Backing Tracks ☐ Group Work ☐ Research
☐ Other: _____

TEACHER / ASSIGNMENTS / IMPROVEMENTS

_____
_____
_____
_____
_____

PROGRESS SNAPSHOT (Circle how today's practice went:)

☹ 🙁 😐 🙂 😀

NEXT PRACTICE GOALS

_____
_____
_____
_____
_____

DAY SESSION

PRACTICE SESSION

DAY / DATE: _____ INSTRUMENT _____
Motivation: ☐ Low ☐ Medium ☐ High

TODAY'S FOCUS
1. _____
2. _____
3. _____

PRACTICE TIME
Planned: ☐ 10 ☐ 20 ☐ 30 ☐ 45 ☐ 60+ minutes   Actual Practice: _____

WHAT YOU PRACTICED TODAY

PLAYING: ☐ New Music ☐ Repertoire ☐ Excerpt Practice ☐ Riffs & Solos ☐ Improvisation
☐ Other: _____

TECHNIQUE & SKILLS: ☐ Scales ☐ Chords ☐ Arpeggios ☐ Ear Training ☐ Exercises
☐ Rhythm & Reading ☐ Applied Theory ☐ Other: _____

CREATIVITY: ☐ Songwriting ☐ Composition ☐ Improvisation ☐ Listening & Study ☐ Lyrics
☐ Other: _____

PERFORMANCE & PROJECTS: ☐ Recording ☐ Backing Tracks ☐ Group Work ☐ Research
☐ Other: _____

TEACHER / ASSIGNMENTS / IMPROVEMENTS
_____
_____
_____
_____
_____

PROGRESS SNAPSHOT (Circle how today's practice went:)

☹   🙁   😐   🙂   😄

NEXT PRACTICE GOALS
_____
_____
_____

DAILY TIP:
Use a timer for short, intense bursts of practice to focus on a specific goal.

PRACTICE SESSION

DAY / DATE: _____   INSTRUMENT _____

Motivation: ☐ Low   ☐ Medium   ☐ High

TODAY'S FOCUS

1. _____
2. _____
3. _____

PRACTICE TIME

Planned: ☐ 10   ☐ 20   ☐ 30   ☐ 45   ☐ 60+ minutes   Actual Practice: _____

WHAT YOU PRACTICED TODAY

PLAYING: ☐ New Music ☐ Repertoire ☐ Excerpt Practice ☐ Riffs & Solos ☐ Improvisation
☐ Other: _____

TECHNIQUE & SKILLS: ☐ Scales ☐ Chords ☐ Arpeggios ☐ Ear Training ☐ Exercises
☐ Rhythm & Reading ☐ Applied Theory ☐ Other: _____

CREATIVITY: ☐ Songwriting ☐ Composition ☐ Improvisation ☐ Listening & Study ☐ Lyrics
☐ Other: _____

PERFORMANCE & PROJECTS: ☐ Recording ☐ Backing Tracks ☐ Group Work ☐ Research
☐ Other: _____

TEACHER / ASSIGNMENTS / IMPROVEMENTS

_____
_____
_____
_____
_____

PROGRESS SNAPSHOT (Circle how today's practice went:)

☹   🙁   😐   🙂   😄

NEXT PRACTICE GOALS

_____
_____
_____
_____
_____

PRACTICE SESSION

DAY / DATE: _____   INSTRUMENT _____

Motivation: ☐ Low   ☐ Medium   ☐ High

TODAY'S FOCUS

1. _____
2. _____
3. _____

PRACTICE TIME

Planned: ☐ 10   ☐ 20   ☐ 30   ☐ 45   ☐ 60+ minutes   Actual Practice: _____

WHAT YOU PRACTICED TODAY

PLAYING: ☐ New Music   ☐ Repertoire   ☐ Excerpt Practice   ☐ Riffs & Solos   ☐ Improvisation
☐ Other: _____

TECHNIQUE & SKILLS: ☐ Scales   ☐ Chords   ☐ Arpeggios   ☐ Ear Training   ☐ Exercises
☐ Rhythm & Reading   ☐ Applied Theory   ☐ Other: _____

CREATIVITY: ☐ Songwriting   ☐ Composition   ☐ Improvisation   ☐ Listening & Study   ☐ Lyrics
☐ Other: _____

PERFORMANCE & PROJECTS: ☐ Recording   ☐ Backing Tracks   ☐ Group Work   ☐ Research
☐ Other: _____

TEACHER / ASSIGNMENTS / IMPROVEMENTS

_____
_____
_____
_____
_____

PROGRESS SNAPSHOT (Circle how today's practice went:)

😠   ☹   😐   🙂   😄

NEXT PRACTICE GOALS

_____
_____
_____

DAILY TIP:

Identify and remove distractions (such as your phone) to improve concentration.

PRACTICE SUMMARY

DATE RANGE: _____

TOTAL SESSIONS: _____ TOTAL TIME: _____

OVERALL FOCUS / ENERGY THIS PERIOD
☐ Strong Momentum ☐ Balanced Progress ☐ Slower Week ☐ Reset / Recovery

TOP 3 ACCOMPLISHMENTS
1. _____
2. _____
3. _____

WHAT YOU WORKED ON MOST

PLAYING: _____

TECHNIQUE & SKILLS: _____

CREATIVITY: _____

PERFORMANCE & PROJECTS: _____

DEEP PRACTICE RECAP
Piece / Exercise: _____
Current Metronome: _____ bpm   Goal: _____ bpm
Focus Area: ☐ Tone ☐ Timing ☐ Fingering ☐ Articulation ☐ Other
Improvement Plan: _____

PERFORMANCES
☐ Recorded / Video ☐ Played for Someone ☐ Ensemble / Jam ☐ None this Week

PROGRESS & INSIGHTS
What improved the most? _____
What still needs work? _____
Creative discoveries or ideas? _____

NEXT FOCUS / UPCOMING GOALS
_____
_____
_____

WEEKLY INSIGHT
Nothing is a waste of time if you use the experience wisely. Auguste Rodin

TEACHER / LESSON NOTES

LESSON DATE: _____ INSTRUMENT _____
Readiness: ☐ Low   ☐ Medium   ☐ High

ASSIGNMENTS / FOCUS POINTS

1. _____
2. _____
3. _____
4. _____
5. _____

HOW LONG YOU SHOULD PRACTICE AT EACH SESSION

Planned: ☐ 10 ☐ 20 ☐ 30 ☐ 45 ☐ 60+ minutes   Other: _____

TECHNIQUE & SKILLS: ☐ Scales ☐ Chords ☐ Arpeggios ☐ Ear Training ☐ Exercises
☐ Rhythm & Reading ☐ Applied Theory ☐ Other: _____
_____
_____

REPERTOIRE 1
Title / Section: _____
Measures / Focus: _____   Tempo Goal: _____ bpm

REPERTOIRE 2
Title / Section: _____
Measures / Focus: _____   Tempo Goal: _____ bpm

REPERTOIRE 3
Title / Section: _____
Measures / Focus: _____   Tempo Goal: _____ bpm

TEACHER COMMENTS
_____
_____
_____
_____
_____

STUDENT NOTES
_____
_____
_____

IDEAS & NOTES

PRACTICE SESSION

DAY / DATE: _____ INSTRUMENT _____
Motivation: ☐ Low ☐ Medium ☐ High

TODAY'S FOCUS

1. _____
2. _____
3. _____

PRACTICE TIME

Planned: ☐ 10 ☐ 20 ☐ 30 ☐ 45 ☐ 60+ minutes   Actual Practice: _____

WHAT YOU PRACTICED TODAY

PLAYING: ☐ New Music ☐ Repertoire ☐ Excerpt Practice ☐ Riffs & Solos ☐ Improvisation
☐ Other: _____

TECHNIQUE & SKILLS: ☐ Scales ☐ Chords ☐ Arpeggios ☐ Ear Training ☐ Exercises
☐ Rhythm & Reading ☐ Applied Theory ☐ Other: _____

CREATIVITY: ☐ Songwriting ☐ Composition ☐ Improvisation ☐ Listening & Study ☐ Lyrics
☐ Other: _____

PERFORMANCE & PROJECTS: ☐ Recording ☐ Backing Tracks ☐ Group Work ☐ Research
☐ Other: _____

TEACHER / ASSIGNMENTS / IMPROVEMENTS

_____
_____
_____
_____
_____

PROGRESS SNAPSHOT (Circle how today's practice went:)

☹   🙁   😐   🙂   😄

NEXT PRACTICE GOALS

_____
_____
_____

DAILY TIP:

Break challenging music into smaller sections and play very slowly.

PRACTICE SESSION

DAY / DATE: _____ INSTRUMENT _____
Motivation: ☐ Low ☐ Medium ☐ High

TODAY'S FOCUS
1. _____
2. _____
3. _____

PRACTICE TIME
Planned: ☐ 10 ☐ 20 ☐ 30 ☐ 45 ☐ 60+ minutes   Actual Practice: _____

WHAT YOU PRACTICED TODAY

PLAYING: ☐ New Music ☐ Repertoire ☐ Excerpt Practice ☐ Riffs & Solos ☐ Improvisation
☐ Other: _____

TECHNIQUE & SKILLS: ☐ Scales ☐ Chords ☐ Arpeggios ☐ Ear Training ☐ Exercises
☐ Rhythm & Reading ☐ Applied Theory ☐ Other: _____

CREATIVITY: ☐ Songwriting ☐ Composition ☐ Improvisation ☐ Listening & Study ☐ Lyrics
☐ Other: _____

PERFORMANCE & PROJECTS: ☐ Recording ☐ Backing Tracks ☐ Group Work ☐ Research
☐ Other: _____

TEACHER / ASSIGNMENTS / IMPROVEMENTS
_____
_____
_____
_____
_____

PROGRESS SNAPSHOT (Circle how today's practice went:)

☹ ☹ 😐 🙂 😊

NEXT PRACTICE GOALS
_____
_____
_____
_____
_____

DAY SESSION

PRACTICE SESSION

DAY / DATE: _____ INSTRUMENT _____
Motivation: ☐ Low ☐ Medium ☐ High

TODAY'S FOCUS

1. _____
2. _____
3. _____

PRACTICE TIME

Planned: ☐ 10 ☐ 20 ☐ 30 ☐ 45 ☐ 60+ minutes   Actual Practice: _____

WHAT YOU PRACTICED TODAY

PLAYING: ☐ New Music ☐ Repertoire ☐ Excerpt Practice ☐ Riffs & Solos ☐ Improvisation
☐ Other: _____

TECHNIQUE & SKILLS: ☐ Scales ☐ Chords ☐ Arpeggios ☐ Ear Training ☐ Exercises
☐ Rhythm & Reading ☐ Applied Theory ☐ Other: _____

CREATIVITY: ☐ Songwriting ☐ Composition ☐ Improvisation ☐ Listening & Study ☐ Lyrics
☐ Other: _____

PERFORMANCE & PROJECTS: ☐ Recording ☐ Backing Tracks ☐ Group Work ☐ Research
☐ Other: _____

TEACHER / ASSIGNMENTS / IMPROVEMENTS

_____
_____
_____
_____
_____

PROGRESS SNAPSHOT (Circle how today's practice went:)

😠   ☹️   😐   🙂   😄

NEXT PRACTICE GOALS

_____
_____
_____

DAILY TIP:

Start every session with a warmup to get your fingers, hands, and arms moving smoothly.

PRACTICE SESSION

DAY / DATE: _____ INSTRUMENT _____
Motivation: ☐ Low ☐ Medium ☐ High

TODAY'S FOCUS
1. _____
2. _____
3. _____

PRACTICE TIME
Planned: ☐ 10 ☐ 20 ☐ 30 ☐ 45 ☐ 60+ minutes   Actual Practice: _____

WHAT YOU PRACTICED TODAY

PLAYING: ☐ New Music ☐ Repertoire ☐ Excerpt Practice ☐ Riffs & Solos ☐ Improvisation
☐ Other: _____

TECHNIQUE & SKILLS: ☐ Scales ☐ Chords ☐ Arpeggios ☐ Ear Training ☐ Exercises
☐ Rhythm & Reading ☐ Applied Theory ☐ Other: _____

CREATIVITY: ☐ Songwriting ☐ Composition ☐ Improvisation ☐ Listening & Study ☐ Lyrics
☐ Other: _____

PERFORMANCE & PROJECTS: ☐ Recording ☐ Backing Tracks ☐ Group Work ☐ Research
☐ Other: _____

TEACHER / ASSIGNMENTS / IMPROVEMENTS
_____
_____
_____
_____
_____

PROGRESS SNAPSHOT (Circle how today's practice went:)

☹ 🙁 😐 🙂 😄

NEXT PRACTICE GOALS
_____
_____
_____
_____
_____

PRACTICE SESSION

DAY / DATE: _____ INSTRUMENT _____
Motivation: ☐ Low ☐ Medium ☐ High

TODAY'S FOCUS

1. _____
2. _____
3. _____

PRACTICE TIME

Planned: ☐ 10 ☐ 20 ☐ 30 ☐ 45 ☐ 60+ minutes   Actual Practice: _____

WHAT YOU PRACTICED TODAY

PLAYING: ☐ New Music ☐ Repertoire ☐ Excerpt Practice ☐ Riffs & Solos ☐ Improvisation
☐ Other: _____

TECHNIQUE & SKILLS: ☐ Scales ☐ Chords ☐ Arpeggios ☐ Ear Training ☐ Exercises
☐ Rhythm & Reading ☐ Applied Theory ☐ Other: _____

CREATIVITY: ☐ Songwriting ☐ Composition ☐ Improvisation ☐ Listening & Study ☐ Lyrics
☐ Other: _____

PERFORMANCE & PROJECTS: ☐ Recording ☐ Backing Tracks ☐ Group Work ☐ Research
☐ Other: _____

TEACHER / ASSIGNMENTS / IMPROVEMENTS

_____
_____
_____
_____
_____

PROGRESS SNAPSHOT (Circle how today's practice went:)

☹ 🙁 😐 🙂 😄

NEXT PRACTICE GOALS

_____
_____
_____

DAILY TIP:

Review your goals regularly to ensure you stay on track and are S.O.U.N.D.

PRACTICE SUMMARY

DATE RANGE: _____
TOTAL SESSIONS: _____ TOTAL TIME: _____

OVERALL FOCUS / ENERGY THIS PERIOD
☐ Strong Momentum ☐ Balanced Progress ☐ Slower Week ☐ Reset / Recovery

TOP 3 ACCOMPLISHMENTS
1. _____
2. _____
3. _____

WHAT YOU WORKED ON MOST
PLAYING: _____
_____

TECHNIQUE & SKILLS: _____
_____

CREATIVITY: _____
_____

PERFORMANCE & PROJECTS: _____
_____

DEEP PRACTICE RECAP
Piece / Exercise: _____
Current Metronome: _____ bpm   Goal: _____ bpm
Focus Area: ☐ Tone ☐ Timing ☐ Fingering ☐ Articulation ☐ Other
Improvement Plan: _____

PERFORMANCES
☐ Recorded / Video ☐ Played for Someone ☐ Ensemble / Jam ☐ None this Week

PROGRESS & INSIGHTS
What improved the most? _____
What still needs work? _____
Creative discoveries or ideas? _____

NEXT FOCUS / UPCOMING GOALS
_____
_____
_____

WEEKLY INSIGHT
Look back at the mistake you loved repeating this week. What did it teach you?

WEEK SUMMARY

PRACTICE SESSION

DAY / DATE: _____ INSTRUMENT _____
Motivation: ☐ Low   ☐ Medium   ☐ High

TODAY'S FOCUS

1. _____
2. _____
3. _____

PRACTICE TIME

Planned: ☐ 10   ☐ 20   ☐ 30   ☐ 45   ☐ 60+ minutes   Actual Practice: _____

WHAT YOU PRACTICED TODAY

PLAYING: ☐ New Music ☐ Repertoire ☐ Excerpt Practice ☐ Riffs & Solos ☐ Improvisation
☐ Other: _____

TECHNIQUE & SKILLS: ☐ Scales ☐ Chords ☐ Arpeggios ☐ Ear Training ☐ Exercises
☐ Rhythm & Reading ☐ Applied Theory ☐ Other: _____

CREATIVITY: ☐ Songwriting ☐ Composition ☐ Improvisation ☐ Listening & Study ☐ Lyrics
☐ Other: _____

PERFORMANCE & PROJECTS: ☐ Recording ☐ Backing Tracks ☐ Group Work ☐ Research
☐ Other: _____

TEACHER / ASSIGNMENTS / IMPROVEMENTS

_____
_____
_____
_____
_____

PROGRESS SNAPSHOT (Circle how today's practice went:)

☹   🙁   😐   🙂   😄

NEXT PRACTICE GOALS

_____
_____
_____

DAILY TIP:

Motivate yourself by planning a reward after a good practice or successful performance.

PRACTICE SESSION

DAY / DATE: _____ INSTRUMENT _____
Motivation: ☐ Low ☐ Medium ☐ High

TODAY'S FOCUS
1. _____
2. _____
3. _____

PRACTICE TIME
Planned: ☐ 10 ☐ 20 ☐ 30 ☐ 45 ☐ 60+ minutes   Actual Practice: _____

WHAT YOU PRACTICED TODAY

PLAYING: ☐ New Music ☐ Repertoire ☐ Excerpt Practice ☐ Riffs & Solos ☐ Improvisation
☐ Other: _____

TECHNIQUE & SKILLS: ☐ Scales ☐ Chords ☐ Arpeggios ☐ Ear Training ☐ Exercises
☐ Rhythm & Reading ☐ Applied Theory ☐ Other: _____

CREATIVITY: ☐ Songwriting ☐ Composition ☐ Improvisation ☐ Listening & Study ☐ Lyrics
☐ Other: _____

PERFORMANCE & PROJECTS: ☐ Recording ☐ Backing Tracks ☐ Group Work ☐ Research
☐ Other: _____

TEACHER / ASSIGNMENTS / IMPROVEMENTS

_____
_____
_____
_____
_____

PROGRESS SNAPSHOT (Circle how today's practice went:)

😠   ☹️   😐   🙂   😄

NEXT PRACTICE GOALS

_____
_____
_____
_____
_____

PRACTICE SESSION

DAY / DATE: _____ INSTRUMENT _____
Motivation: ☐ Low ☐ Medium ☐ High

TODAY'S FOCUS

1. _____
2. _____
3. _____

PRACTICE TIME

Planned: ☐ 10 ☐ 20 ☐ 30 ☐ 45 ☐ 60+ minutes   Actual Practice: _____

WHAT YOU PRACTICED TODAY

PLAYING: ☐ New Music ☐ Repertoire ☐ Excerpt Practice ☐ Riffs & Solos ☐ Improvisation
☐ Other: _____

TECHNIQUE & SKILLS: ☐ Scales ☐ Chords ☐ Arpeggios ☐ Ear Training ☐ Exercises
☐ Rhythm & Reading ☐ Applied Theory ☐ Other: _____

CREATIVITY: ☐ Songwriting ☐ Composition ☐ Improvisation ☐ Listening & Study ☐ Lyrics
☐ Other: _____

PERFORMANCE & PROJECTS: ☐ Recording ☐ Backing Tracks ☐ Group Work ☐ Research
☐ Other: _____

TEACHER / ASSIGNMENTS / IMPROVEMENTS

_____
_____
_____
_____
_____

PROGRESS SNAPSHOT (Circle how today's practice went:)

😠   ☹️   😐   🙂   😄

NEXT PRACTICE GOALS

_____
_____
_____

DAILY TIP:

Set a deadline to maintain focus on your musical goal.

PRACTICE SESSION

DAY / DATE: _____ INSTRUMENT _____
Motivation: ☐ Low ☐ Medium ☐ High

TODAY'S FOCUS
1. _____
2. _____
3. _____

PRACTICE TIME
Planned: ☐ 10 ☐ 20 ☐ 30 ☐ 45 ☐ 60+ minutes   Actual Practice: _____

WHAT YOU PRACTICED TODAY

PLAYING: ☐ New Music ☐ Repertoire ☐ Excerpt Practice ☐ Riffs & Solos ☐ Improvisation
☐ Other: _____

TECHNIQUE & SKILLS: ☐ Scales ☐ Chords ☐ Arpeggios ☐ Ear Training ☐ Exercises
☐ Rhythm & Reading ☐ Applied Theory ☐ Other: _____

CREATIVITY: ☐ Songwriting ☐ Composition ☐ Improvisation ☐ Listening & Study ☐ Lyrics
☐ Other: _____

PERFORMANCE & PROJECTS: ☐ Recording ☐ Backing Tracks ☐ Group Work ☐ Research
☐ Other: _____

TEACHER / ASSIGNMENTS / IMPROVEMENTS
_____
_____
_____
_____

PROGRESS SNAPSHOT (Circle how today's practice went:)

😠 ☹ 😐 🙂 😄

NEXT PRACTICE GOALS
_____
_____
_____
_____

DAY SESSION

PRACTICE SESSION

DAY / DATE: _____ INSTRUMENT _____

Motivation: ☐ Low ☐ Medium ☐ High

TODAY'S FOCUS

1. _____
2. _____
3. _____

PRACTICE TIME

Planned: ☐ 10 ☐ 20 ☐ 30 ☐ 45 ☐ 60+ minutes   Actual Practice: _____

WHAT YOU PRACTICED TODAY

PLAYING: ☐ New Music ☐ Repertoire ☐ Excerpt Practice ☐ Riffs & Solos ☐ Improvisation
☐ Other: _____

TECHNIQUE & SKILLS: ☐ Scales ☐ Chords ☐ Arpeggios ☐ Ear Training ☐ Exercises
☐ Rhythm & Reading ☐ Applied Theory ☐ Other: _____

CREATIVITY: ☐ Songwriting ☐ Composition ☐ Improvisation ☐ Listening & Study ☐ Lyrics
☐ Other: _____

PERFORMANCE & PROJECTS: ☐ Recording ☐ Backing Tracks ☐ Group Work ☐ Research
☐ Other: _____

TEACHER / ASSIGNMENTS / IMPROVEMENTS

_____
_____
_____
_____
_____

PROGRESS SNAPSHOT (Circle how today's practice went:)

☹ 🙁 😐 🙂 😄

NEXT PRACTICE GOALS

_____
_____
_____

DAILY TIP:

Set S.O.U.N.D. goals: Simple, Observable, Useful, Natural and Dated.

PRACTICE SUMMARY

DATE RANGE: _____
TOTAL SESSIONS: _____ TOTAL TIME: _____

OVERALL FOCUS / ENERGY THIS PERIOD
☐ Strong Momentum ☐ Balanced Progress ☐ Slower Week ☐ Reset / Recovery

TOP 3 ACCOMPLISHMENTS
1. _____
2. _____
3. _____

WHAT YOU WORKED ON MOST

PLAYING: _____
_____

TECHNIQUE & SKILLS: _____
_____

CREATIVITY: _____
_____

PERFORMANCE & PROJECTS: _____
_____

DEEP PRACTICE RECAP
Piece / Exercise: _____
Current Metronome: _____ bpm   Goal: _____ bpm
Focus Area: ☐ Tone ☐ Timing ☐ Fingering ☐ Articulation ☐ Other
Improvement Plan: _____

PERFORMANCES
☐ Recorded / Video ☐ Played for Someone ☐ Ensemble /Jam ☐ None this Week

PROGRESS & INSIGHTS
What improved the most? _____
What still needs work? _____
Creative discoveries or ideas? _____

NEXT FOCUS / UPCOMING GOALS
_____
_____
_____

WEEKLY INSIGHT
The more closely you look at a thing, the more distant it becomes. Rilke

TEACHER / LESSON NOTES

LESSON DATE: _____ INSTRUMENT _____
Readiness: ☐ Low ☐ Medium ☐ High

ASSIGNMENTS / FOCUS POINTS
1. _____
2. _____
3. _____
4. _____
5. _____

HOW LONG YOU SHOULD PRACTICE AT EACH SESSION
Planned: ☐ 10 ☐ 20 ☐ 30 ☐ 45 ☐ 60+ minutes Other: _____

TECHNIQUE & SKILLS: ☐ Scales ☐ Chords ☐ Arpeggios ☐ Ear Training ☐ Exercises
☐ Rhythm & Reading ☐ Applied Theory ☐ Other: _____
_____
_____

REPERTOIRE 1
Title / Section: _____
Measures / Focus: _____ Tempo Goal: _____ bpm

REPERTOIRE 2
Title / Section: _____
Measures / Focus: _____ Tempo Goal: _____ bpm

REPERTOIRE 3
Title / Section: _____
Measures / Focus: _____ Tempo Goal: _____ bpm

TEACHER COMMENTS
_____
_____
_____
_____
_____

STUDENT NOTES
_____
_____
_____

IDEAS & NOTES

MONTHLY REFLECTION

MONTH: _____ TOTAL TIME: _____
TOTAL SESSIONS: _____ TOTAL PERFORMANCES: _____

RATE YOUR PROGRESS THIS MONTH: BELOW ★ AVERAGE ★ ★ ABOVE ★ ★ ★

WHAT ARE YOU MOST GRATEFUL FOR WITH YOUR MUSIC THIS MONTH

_____
_____
_____
_____
_____

SET YOUR GOALS FOR NEXT MONTH

_____
_____
_____
_____
_____

POSITIVE LESSONS OR HABITS TO CONTINUE NEXT MONTH

_____
_____
_____
_____
_____

NOTES

_____
_____
_____
_____
_____

INSIGHT

Progress is invisible day to day but obvious month to month

PRACTICE SESSION

DAY / DATE: _____ INSTRUMENT _____

Motivation: ☐ Low ☐ Medium ☐ High

TODAY'S FOCUS

1. _____
2. _____
3. _____

PRACTICE TIME

Planned: ☐ 10 ☐ 20 ☐ 30 ☐ 45 ☐ 60+ minutes   Actual Practice: _____

WHAT YOU PRACTICED TODAY

PLAYING: ☐ New Music ☐ Repertoire ☐ Excerpt Practice ☐ Riffs & Solos ☐ Improvisation
☐ Other: _____

TECHNIQUE & SKILLS: ☐ Scales ☐ Chords ☐ Arpeggios ☐ Ear Training ☐ Exercises
☐ Rhythm & Reading ☐ Applied Theory ☐ Other: _____

CREATIVITY: ☐ Songwriting ☐ Composition ☐ Improvisation ☐ Listening & Study ☐ Lyrics
☐ Other: _____

PERFORMANCE & PROJECTS: ☐ Recording ☐ Backing Tracks ☐ Group Work ☐ Research
☐ Other: _____

TEACHER / ASSIGNMENTS / IMPROVEMENTS

_____
_____
_____
_____
_____

PROGRESS SNAPSHOT (Circle how today's practice went:)

☹ 🙁 😐 🙂 😄

NEXT PRACTICE GOALS

_____
_____
_____

DAILY TIP:

Luck is what happens when preparation meets opportunity. Seneca

PRACTICE SESSION

DAY / DATE: _____ INSTRUMENT _____

Motivation: ☐ Low ☐ Medium ☐ High

TODAY'S FOCUS
1. _____
2. _____
3. _____

PRACTICE TIME
Planned: ☐ 10 ☐ 20 ☐ 30 ☐ 45 ☐ 60+ minutes   Actual Practice: _____

WHAT YOU PRACTICED TODAY

PLAYING: ☐ New Music ☐ Repertoire ☐ Excerpt Practice ☐ Riffs & Solos ☐ Improvisation
☐ Other: _____

TECHNIQUE & SKILLS: ☐ Scales ☐ Chords ☐ Arpeggios ☐ Ear Training ☐ Exercises
☐ Rhythm & Reading ☐ Applied Theory ☐ Other: _____

CREATIVITY: ☐ Songwriting ☐ Composition ☐ Improvisation ☐ Listening & Study ☐ Lyrics
☐ Other: _____

PERFORMANCE & PROJECTS: ☐ Recording ☐ Backing Tracks ☐ Group Work ☐ Research
☐ Other: _____

TEACHER / ASSIGNMENTS / IMPROVEMENTS
_____
_____
_____
_____
_____

PROGRESS SNAPSHOT (Circle how today's practice went:)

☹   😕   😐   🙂   😊

NEXT PRACTICE GOALS
_____
_____
_____
_____
_____

DAY SESSION

PRACTICE SESSION

DAY / DATE: _____   INSTRUMENT _____

Motivation: ☐ Low   ☐ Medium   ☐ High

TODAY'S FOCUS

1. _____
2. _____
3. _____

PRACTICE TIME

Planned: ☐ 10   ☐ 20   ☐ 30   ☐ 45   ☐ 60+ minutes   Actual Practice: _____

WHAT YOU PRACTICED TODAY

PLAYING: ☐ New Music   ☐ Repertoire   ☐ Excerpt Practice   ☐ Riffs & Solos   ☐ Improvisation
☐ Other: _____

TECHNIQUE & SKILLS: ☐ Scales   ☐ Chords   ☐ Arpeggios   ☐ Ear Training   ☐ Exercises
☐ Rhythm & Reading   ☐ Applied Theory   ☐ Other: _____

CREATIVITY: ☐ Songwriting   ☐ Composition   ☐ Improvisation   ☐ Listening & Study   ☐ Lyrics
☐ Other: _____

PERFORMANCE & PROJECTS: ☐ Recording   ☐ Backing Tracks   ☐ Group Work   ☐ Research
☐ Other: _____

TEACHER / ASSIGNMENTS / IMPROVEMENTS

_____
_____
_____
_____
_____

PROGRESS SNAPSHOT (Circle how today's practice went:)

😠   ☹   😐   🙂   😄

NEXT PRACTICE GOALS

_____
_____
_____

DAILY TIP:

Plan sessions the night before; one less thing to do when you practice the next day.

PRACTICE SESSION

DAY / DATE: _____ INSTRUMENT _____

Motivation: ☐ Low ☐ Medium ☐ High

TODAY'S FOCUS

1. _____
2. _____
3. _____

PRACTICE TIME

Planned: ☐ 10 ☐ 20 ☐ 30 ☐ 45 ☐ 60+ minutes   Actual Practice: _____

WHAT YOU PRACTICED TODAY

PLAYING: ☐ New Music ☐ Repertoire ☐ Excerpt Practice ☐ Riffs & Solos ☐ Improvisation
☐ Other: _____

TECHNIQUE & SKILLS: ☐ Scales ☐ Chords ☐ Arpeggios ☐ Ear Training ☐ Exercises
☐ Rhythm & Reading ☐ Applied Theory ☐ Other: _____

CREATIVITY: ☐ Songwriting ☐ Composition ☐ Improvisation ☐ Listening & Study ☐ Lyrics
☐ Other: _____

PERFORMANCE & PROJECTS: ☐ Recording ☐ Backing Tracks ☐ Group Work ☐ Research
☐ Other: _____

TEACHER / ASSIGNMENTS / IMPROVEMENTS

_____
_____
_____
_____
_____

PROGRESS SNAPSHOT (Circle how today's practice went:)

☹ 🙁 😐 🙂 😄

NEXT PRACTICE GOALS

_____
_____
_____
_____
_____

DAY SESSION

PRACTICE SESSION

DAY / DATE: _____ INSTRUMENT _____
Motivation: ☐ Low ☐ Medium ☐ High

TODAY'S FOCUS

1. _____
2. _____
3. _____

PRACTICE TIME

Planned: ☐ 10 ☐ 20 ☐ 30 ☐ 45 ☐ 60+ minutes   Actual Practice: _____

WHAT YOU PRACTICED TODAY

PLAYING: ☐ New Music ☐ Repertoire ☐ Excerpt Practice ☐ Riffs & Solos ☐ Improvisation
☐ Other: _____

TECHNIQUE & SKILLS: ☐ Scales ☐ Chords ☐ Arpeggios ☐ Ear Training ☐ Exercises
☐ Rhythm & Reading ☐ Applied Theory ☐ Other: _____

CREATIVITY: ☐ Songwriting ☐ Composition ☐ Improvisation ☐ Listening & Study ☐ Lyrics
☐ Other: _____

PERFORMANCE & PROJECTS: ☐ Recording ☐ Backing Tracks ☐ Group Work ☐ Research
☐ Other: _____

TEACHER / ASSIGNMENTS / IMPROVEMENTS

_____
_____
_____
_____
_____

PROGRESS SNAPSHOT (Circle how today's practice went:)

☹️   🙁   😐   🙂   😄

NEXT PRACTICE GOALS

_____
_____
_____

DAILY TIP:
Set a clear start and stop time; deadlines help focus your attention.

PRACTICE SUMMARY

DATE RANGE: _____
TOTAL SESSIONS: _____ TOTAL TIME: _____

OVERALL FOCUS / ENERGY THIS PERIOD
☐ Strong Momentum ☐ Balanced Progress ☐ Slower Week ☐ Reset / Recovery

TOP 3 ACCOMPLISHMENTS
1. _____
2. _____
3. _____

WHAT YOU WORKED ON MOST
PLAYING: _____
_____

TECHNIQUE & SKILLS: _____
_____

CREATIVITY: _____
_____

PERFORMANCE & PROJECTS: _____
_____

DEEP PRACTICE RECAP
Piece / Exercise: _____
Current Metronome: _____ bpm   Goal: _____ bpm
Focus Area: ☐ Tone ☐ Timing ☐ Fingering ☐ Articulation ☐ Other
Improvement Plan: _____

PERFORMANCES
☐ Recorded / Video ☐ Played for Someone ☐ Ensemble / Jam ☐ None this Week

PROGRESS & INSIGHTS
What improved the most? _____
What still needs work? _____
Creative discoveries or ideas? _____

NEXT FOCUS / UPCOMING GOALS
_____
_____
_____

WEEKLY INSIGHT
Be grateful for what improved most this week, not what still needs work.

PRACTICE SESSION

DAY / DATE: _____ INSTRUMENT _____
Motivation: ☐ Low ☐ Medium ☐ High

TODAY'S FOCUS

1. _____
2. _____
3. _____

PRACTICE TIME

Planned: ☐ 10 ☐ 20 ☐ 30 ☐ 45 ☐ 60+ minutes   Actual Practice: _____

WHAT YOU PRACTICED TODAY

PLAYING: ☐ New Music ☐ Repertoire ☐ Excerpt Practice ☐ Riffs & Solos ☐ Improvisation
☐ Other: _____

TECHNIQUE & SKILLS: ☐ Scales ☐ Chords ☐ Arpeggios ☐ Ear Training ☐ Exercises
☐ Rhythm & Reading ☐ Applied Theory ☐ Other: _____

CREATIVITY: ☐ Songwriting ☐ Composition ☐ Improvisation ☐ Listening & Study ☐ Lyrics
☐ Other: _____

PERFORMANCE & PROJECTS: ☐ Recording ☐ Backing Tracks ☐ Group Work ☐ Research
☐ Other: _____

TEACHER / ASSIGNMENTS / IMPROVEMENTS

_____
_____
_____
_____
_____

PROGRESS SNAPSHOT (Circle how today's practice went:)

☹ ☹ 😐 🙂 😄

NEXT PRACTICE GOALS

_____
_____
_____

DAILY TIP:

When you hit your limits, return to the fundamentals.

PRACTICE SESSION

DAY / DATE: _____ INSTRUMENT _____

Motivation: ☐ Low ☐ Medium ☐ High

TODAY'S FOCUS
1. _____
2. _____
3. _____

PRACTICE TIME
Planned: ☐ 10 ☐ 20 ☐ 30 ☐ 45 ☐ 60+ minutes   Actual Practice: _____

WHAT YOU PRACTICED TODAY

PLAYING: ☐ New Music ☐ Repertoire ☐ Excerpt Practice ☐ Riffs & Solos ☐ Improvisation
☐ Other: _____

TECHNIQUE & SKILLS: ☐ Scales ☐ Chords ☐ Arpeggios ☐ Ear Training ☐ Exercises
☐ Rhythm & Reading ☐ Applied Theory ☐ Other: _____

CREATIVITY: ☐ Songwriting ☐ Composition ☐ Improvisation ☐ Listening & Study ☐ Lyrics
☐ Other: _____

PERFORMANCE & PROJECTS: ☐ Recording ☐ Backing Tracks ☐ Group Work ☐ Research
☐ Other: _____

TEACHER / ASSIGNMENTS / IMPROVEMENTS

_____
_____
_____
_____
_____

PROGRESS SNAPSHOT (Circle how today's practice went:)

😠 😕 😐 🙂 😄

NEXT PRACTICE GOALS

_____
_____
_____
_____
_____

DAY SESSION

PRACTICE SESSION

DAY / DATE: _____ INSTRUMENT _____
Motivation: ☐ Low ☐ Medium ☐ High

TODAY'S FOCUS

1. _____
2. _____
3. _____

PRACTICE TIME

Planned: ☐ 10 ☐ 20 ☐ 30 ☐ 45 ☐ 60+ minutes   Actual Practice: _____

WHAT YOU PRACTICED TODAY

PLAYING: ☐ New Music ☐ Repertoire ☐ Excerpt Practice ☐ Riffs & Solos ☐ Improvisation
☐ Other: _____

TECHNIQUE & SKILLS: ☐ Scales ☐ Chords ☐ Arpeggios ☐ Ear Training ☐ Exercises
☐ Rhythm & Reading ☐ Applied Theory ☐ Other: _____

CREATIVITY: ☐ Songwriting ☐ Composition ☐ Improvisation ☐ Listening & Study ☐ Lyrics
☐ Other: _____

PERFORMANCE & PROJECTS: ☐ Recording ☐ Backing Tracks ☐ Group Work ☐ Research
☐ Other: _____

TEACHER / ASSIGNMENTS / IMPROVEMENTS

_____
_____
_____
_____
_____

PROGRESS SNAPSHOT (Circle how today's practice went:)

☹ 😕 😐 🙂 😄

NEXT PRACTICE GOALS

_____
_____
_____

DAILY TIP:

Keep curiosity louder than criticism.

PRACTICE SESSION

DAY / DATE: _____ INSTRUMENT _____
Motivation: ☐ Low ☐ Medium ☐ High

TODAY'S FOCUS
1. _____
2. _____
3. _____

PRACTICE TIME
Planned: ☐ 10 ☐ 20 ☐ 30 ☐ 45 ☐ 60+ minutes   Actual Practice: _____

WHAT YOU PRACTICED TODAY

PLAYING: ☐ New Music ☐ Repertoire ☐ Excerpt Practice ☐ Riffs & Solos ☐ Improvisation
☐ Other: _____

TECHNIQUE & SKILLS: ☐ Scales ☐ Chords ☐ Arpeggios ☐ Ear Training ☐ Exercises
☐ Rhythm & Reading ☐ Applied Theory ☐ Other: _____

CREATIVITY: ☐ Songwriting ☐ Composition ☐ Improvisation ☐ Listening & Study ☐ Lyrics
☐ Other: _____

PERFORMANCE & PROJECTS: ☐ Recording ☐ Backing Tracks ☐ Group Work ☐ Research
☐ Other: _____

TEACHER / ASSIGNMENTS / IMPROVEMENTS
_____
_____
_____
_____
_____

PROGRESS SNAPSHOT (Circle how today's practice went:)

☹ 🙁 😐 🙂 😀

NEXT PRACTICE GOALS
_____
_____
_____
_____
_____

DAY SESSION

PRACTICE SESSION

DAY / DATE: _____ INSTRUMENT _____

Motivation: ☐ Low ☐ Medium ☐ High

TODAY'S FOCUS

1. _____
2. _____
3. _____

PRACTICE TIME

Planned: ☐ 10 ☐ 20 ☐ 30 ☐ 45 ☐ 60+ minutes   Actual Practice: _____

WHAT YOU PRACTICED TODAY

PLAYING: ☐ New Music ☐ Repertoire ☐ Excerpt Practice ☐ Riffs & Solos ☐ Improvisation
☐ Other: _____

TECHNIQUE & SKILLS: ☐ Scales ☐ Chords ☐ Arpeggios ☐ Ear Training ☐ Exercises
☐ Rhythm & Reading ☐ Applied Theory ☐ Other: _____

_____

CREATIVITY: ☐ Songwriting ☐ Composition ☐ Improvisation ☐ Listening & Study ☐ Lyrics
☐ Other: _____

PERFORMANCE & PROJECTS: ☐ Recording ☐ Backing Tracks ☐ Group Work ☐ Research
☐ Other: _____

TEACHER / ASSIGNMENTS / IMPROVEMENTS

_____
_____
_____
_____
_____

PROGRESS SNAPSHOT (Circle how today's practice went:)

😠 ☹️ 😐 🙂 😄

NEXT PRACTICE GOALS

_____
_____
_____

DAILY TIP:

Make every practice session begin with a meaningful breath.

PRACTICE SUMMARY

DATE RANGE: _____
TOTAL SESSIONS: _____ TOTAL TIME: _____

OVERALL FOCUS / ENERGY THIS PERIOD
☐ Strong Momentum ☐ Balanced Progress ☐ Slower Week ☐ Reset / Recovery

TOP 3 ACCOMPLISHMENTS
1. _____
2. _____
3. _____

WHAT YOU WORKED ON MOST
PLAYING: _____
_____

TECHNIQUE & SKILLS: _____
_____

CREATIVITY: _____
_____

PERFORMANCE & PROJECTS: _____
_____

DEEP PRACTICE RECAP
Piece / Exercise: _____
Current Metronome: _____ bpm   Goal: _____ bpm
Focus Area: ☐ Tone ☐ Timing ☐ Fingering ☐ Articulation ☐ Other
Improvement Plan: _____

PERFORMANCES
☐ Recorded / Video ☐ Played for Someone ☐ Ensemble / Jam ☐ None this Week

PROGRESS & INSIGHTS
What improved the most? _____
What still needs work? _____
Creative discoveries or ideas? _____

NEXT FOCUS / UPCOMING GOALS
_____
_____
_____

WEEKLY INSIGHT
Revisit one old piece and notice how differently it feels to play now.

TEACHER / LESSON NOTES

LESSON DATE: _____ INSTRUMENT _____
Readiness: ☐ Low ☐ Medium ☐ High

ASSIGNMENTS / FOCUS POINTS

1. _____
2. _____
3. _____
4. _____
5. _____

HOW LONG YOU SHOULD PRACTICE AT EACH SESSION

Planned: ☐ 10 ☐ 20 ☐ 30 ☐ 45 ☐ 60+ minutes Other: _____

TECHNIQUE & SKILLS: ☐ Scales ☐ Chords ☐ Arpeggios ☐ Ear Training ☐ Exercises
☐ Rhythm & Reading ☐ Applied Theory ☐ Other: _____
_____
_____

REPERTOIRE 1
Title / Section: _____
Measures / Focus: _____ Tempo Goal: _____ bpm

REPERTOIRE 2
Title / Section: _____
Measures / Focus: _____ Tempo Goal: _____ bpm

REPERTOIRE 3
Title / Section: _____
Measures / Focus: _____ Tempo Goal: _____ bpm

TEACHER COMMENTS
_____
_____
_____
_____
_____

STUDENT NOTES
_____
_____
_____

IDEAS & NOTES

PRACTICE SESSION

DAY / DATE: _____ INSTRUMENT _____
Motivation: ☐ Low   ☐ Medium   ☐ High

TODAY'S FOCUS

1. _____
2. _____
3. _____

PRACTICE TIME

Planned: ☐ 10 ☐ 20 ☐ 30 ☐ 45 ☐ 60+ minutes   Actual Practice: _____

WHAT YOU PRACTICED TODAY

PLAYING: ☐ New Music ☐ Repertoire ☐ Excerpt Practice ☐ Riffs & Solos ☐ Improvisation
☐ Other: _____

TECHNIQUE & SKILLS: ☐ Scales ☐ Chords ☐ Arpeggios ☐ Ear Training ☐ Exercises
☐ Rhythm & Reading ☐ Applied Theory ☐ Other: _____

CREATIVITY: ☐ Songwriting ☐ Composition ☐ Improvisation ☐ Listening & Study ☐ Lyrics
☐ Other: _____

PERFORMANCE & PROJECTS: ☐ Recording ☐ Backing Tracks ☐ Group Work ☐ Research
☐ Other: _____

TEACHER / ASSIGNMENTS / IMPROVEMENTS

_____
_____
_____
_____
_____

PROGRESS SNAPSHOT (Circle how today's practice went:)

☹ 🙁 😐 🙂 😄

NEXT PRACTICE GOALS

_____
_____
_____

DAILY TIP:

Practice in the dark, or with your eyes closed, to trust your muscle memory over your visual sight.

PRACTICE SESSION

DAY / DATE: _____ INSTRUMENT _____
Motivation: ☐ Low ☐ Medium ☐ High

TODAY'S FOCUS
1. _____
2. _____
3. _____

PRACTICE TIME
Planned: ☐ 10 ☐ 20 ☐ 30 ☐ 45 ☐ 60+ minutes   Actual Practice: _____

WHAT YOU PRACTICED TODAY

PLAYING: ☐ New Music ☐ Repertoire ☐ Excerpt Practice ☐ Riffs & Solos ☐ Improvisation
☐ Other: _____

TECHNIQUE & SKILLS: ☐ Scales ☐ Chords ☐ Arpeggios ☐ Ear Training ☐ Exercises
☐ Rhythm & Reading ☐ Applied Theory ☐ Other: _____

CREATIVITY: ☐ Songwriting ☐ Composition ☐ Improvisation ☐ Listening & Study ☐ Lyrics
☐ Other: _____

PERFORMANCE & PROJECTS: ☐ Recording ☐ Backing Tracks ☐ Group Work ☐ Research
☐ Other: _____

TEACHER / ASSIGNMENTS / IMPROVEMENTS
_____
_____
_____
_____
_____

PROGRESS SNAPSHOT (Circle how today's practice went:)

😠   ☹️   😐   🙂   😄

NEXT PRACTICE GOALS
_____
_____
_____
_____
_____

DAY SESSION

PRACTICE SESSION

DAY / DATE: _____ INSTRUMENT _____
Motivation: ☐ Low ☐ Medium ☐ High

TODAY'S FOCUS

1. _____
2. _____
3. _____

PRACTICE TIME

Planned: ☐ 10 ☐ 20 ☐ 30 ☐ 45 ☐ 60+ minutes   Actual Practice: _____

WHAT YOU PRACTICED TODAY

PLAYING: ☐ New Music ☐ Repertoire ☐ Excerpt Practice ☐ Riffs & Solos ☐ Improvisation
☐ Other: _____

TECHNIQUE & SKILLS: ☐ Scales ☐ Chords ☐ Arpeggios ☐ Ear Training ☐ Exercises
☐ Rhythm & Reading ☐ Applied Theory ☐ Other: _____

CREATIVITY: ☐ Songwriting ☐ Composition ☐ Improvisation ☐ Listening & Study ☐ Lyrics
☐ Other: _____

PERFORMANCE & PROJECTS: ☐ Recording ☐ Backing Tracks ☐ Group Work ☐ Research
☐ Other: _____

TEACHER / ASSIGNMENTS / IMPROVEMENTS

_____
_____
_____
_____
_____

PROGRESS SNAPSHOT (Circle how today's practice went:)

☹ 🙁 😐 🙂 😄

NEXT PRACTICE GOALS

_____
_____
_____

DAILY TIP:
Time is the musician's canvas. Rimsky-Korsakov

PRACTICE SESSION

DAY / DATE: _____ INSTRUMENT _____
Motivation: ☐ Low ☐ Medium ☐ High

TODAY'S FOCUS
1. _____
2. _____
3. _____

PRACTICE TIME
Planned: ☐ 10 ☐ 20 ☐ 30 ☐ 45 ☐ 60+ minutes   Actual Practice: _____

WHAT YOU PRACTICED TODAY

PLAYING: ☐ New Music ☐ Repertoire ☐ Excerpt Practice ☐ Riffs & Solos ☐ Improvisation
☐ Other: _____

TECHNIQUE & SKILLS: ☐ Scales ☐ Chords ☐ Arpeggios ☐ Ear Training ☐ Exercises
☐ Rhythm & Reading ☐ Applied Theory ☐ Other: _____

CREATIVITY: ☐ Songwriting ☐ Composition ☐ Improvisation ☐ Listening & Study ☐ Lyrics
☐ Other: _____

PERFORMANCE & PROJECTS: ☐ Recording ☐ Backing Tracks ☐ Group Work ☐ Research
☐ Other: _____

TEACHER / ASSIGNMENTS / IMPROVEMENTS
_____
_____
_____
_____
_____

PROGRESS SNAPSHOT (Circle how today's practice went:)

☹ 🙁 😐 🙂 😄

NEXT PRACTICE GOALS
_____
_____
_____
_____
_____

DAY SESSION

PRACTICE SESSION

DAY / DATE: _____ INSTRUMENT _____
Motivation: ☐ Low ☐ Medium ☐ High

TODAY'S FOCUS

1. _____
2. _____
3. _____

PRACTICE TIME

Planned: ☐ 10 ☐ 20 ☐ 30 ☐ 45 ☐ 60+ minutes   Actual Practice: _____

WHAT YOU PRACTICED TODAY

PLAYING: ☐ New Music ☐ Repertoire ☐ Excerpt Practice ☐ Riffs & Solos ☐ Improvisation
☐ Other: _____

TECHNIQUE & SKILLS: ☐ Scales ☐ Chords ☐ Arpeggios ☐ Ear Training ☐ Exercises
☐ Rhythm & Reading ☐ Applied Theory ☐ Other: _____

CREATIVITY: ☐ Songwriting ☐ Composition ☐ Improvisation ☐ Listening & Study ☐ Lyrics
☐ Other: _____

PERFORMANCE & PROJECTS: ☐ Recording ☐ Backing Tracks ☐ Group Work ☐ Research
☐ Other: _____

TEACHER / ASSIGNMENTS / IMPROVEMENTS

_____
_____
_____
_____
_____

PROGRESS SNAPSHOT (Circle how today's practice went:)

☹ 😕 😐 🙂 😄

NEXT PRACTICE GOALS

_____
_____
_____

DAILY TIP:

The purpose of technique is freedom. Artur Schnabel

PRACTICE SUMMARY

DATE RANGE: _____

TOTAL SESSIONS: _____ TOTAL TIME: _____

OVERALL FOCUS / ENERGY THIS PERIOD
☐ Strong Momentum ☐ Balanced Progress ☐ Slower Week ☐ Reset / Recovery

TOP 3 ACCOMPLISHMENTS
1. _____
2. _____
3. _____

WHAT YOU WORKED ON MOST

PLAYING: _____
_____

TECHNIQUE & SKILLS: _____
_____

CREATIVITY: _____
_____

PERFORMANCE & PROJECTS: _____
_____

DEEP PRACTICE RECAP
Piece / Exercise: _____
Current Metronome: _____ bpm   Goal: _____ bpm
Focus Area: ☐ Tone ☐ Timing ☐ Fingering ☐ Articulation ☐ Other
Improvement Plan: _____

PERFORMANCES
☐ Recorded / Video ☐ Played for Someone ☐ Ensemble /Jam ☐ None this Week

PROGRESS & INSIGHTS
What improved the most? _____
What still needs work? _____
Creative discoveries or ideas? _____

NEXT FOCUS / UPCOMING GOALS
_____
_____
_____

WEEKLY INSIGHT
Dedicate one day to reviewing fundamentals; strong roots grow new ideas.

PRACTICE SESSION

DAY / DATE: _____ INSTRUMENT _____
Motivation: ☐ Low ☐ Medium ☐ High

TODAY'S FOCUS

1. _____
2. _____
3. _____

PRACTICE TIME

Planned: ☐ 10 ☐ 20 ☐ 30 ☐ 45 ☐ 60+ minutes   Actual Practice: _____

WHAT YOU PRACTICED TODAY

PLAYING: ☐ New Music ☐ Repertoire ☐ Excerpt Practice ☐ Riffs & Solos ☐ Improvisation
☐ Other: _____

TECHNIQUE & SKILLS: ☐ Scales ☐ Chords ☐ Arpeggios ☐ Ear Training ☐ Exercises
☐ Rhythm & Reading ☐ Applied Theory ☐ Other: _____

CREATIVITY: ☐ Songwriting ☐ Composition ☐ Improvisation ☐ Listening & Study ☐ Lyrics
☐ Other: _____

PERFORMANCE & PROJECTS: ☐ Recording ☐ Backing Tracks ☐ Group Work ☐ Research
☐ Other: _____

TEACHER / ASSIGNMENTS / IMPROVEMENTS

_____
_____
_____
_____
_____

PROGRESS SNAPSHOT (Circle how today's practice went:)

😠   ☹️   😐   🙂   😃

NEXT PRACTICE GOALS

_____
_____
_____

DAILY TIP:

Passion outweighs precision. Ludwig van Beethoven.

PRACTICE SESSION

DAY / DATE: _____ INSTRUMENT _____

Motivation: ☐ Low ☐ Medium ☐ High

TODAY'S FOCUS
1. _____
2. _____
3. _____

PRACTICE TIME
Planned: ☐ 10 ☐ 20 ☐ 30 ☐ 45 ☐ 60+ minutes   Actual Practice: _____

WHAT YOU PRACTICED TODAY

PLAYING: ☐ New Music ☐ Repertoire ☐ Excerpt Practice ☐ Riffs & Solos ☐ Improvisation
☐ Other: _____

TECHNIQUE & SKILLS: ☐ Scales ☐ Chords ☐ Arpeggios ☐ Ear Training ☐ Exercises
☐ Rhythm & Reading ☐ Applied Theory ☐ Other: _____

CREATIVITY: ☐ Songwriting ☐ Composition ☐ Improvisation ☐ Listening & Study ☐ Lyrics
☐ Other: _____

PERFORMANCE & PROJECTS: ☐ Recording ☐ Backing Tracks ☐ Group Work ☐ Research
☐ Other: _____

TEACHER / ASSIGNMENTS / IMPROVEMENTS
_____
_____
_____
_____
_____

PROGRESS SNAPSHOT (Circle how today's practice went:)

☹ 🙁 😐 🙂 😄

NEXT PRACTICE GOALS
_____
_____
_____
_____
_____

DAY SESSION

PRACTICE SESSION

DAY / DATE: _____ INSTRUMENT _____

Motivation: ☐ Low ☐ Medium ☐ High

TODAY'S FOCUS

1. _____
2. _____
3. _____

PRACTICE TIME

Planned: ☐ 10 ☐ 20 ☐ 30 ☐ 45 ☐ 60+ minutes   Actual Practice: _____

WHAT YOU PRACTICED TODAY

PLAYING: ☐ New Music ☐ Repertoire ☐ Excerpt Practice ☐ Riffs & Solos ☐ Improvisation
☐ Other: _____

TECHNIQUE & SKILLS: ☐ Scales ☐ Chords ☐ Arpeggios ☐ Ear Training ☐ Exercises
☐ Rhythm & Reading ☐ Applied Theory ☐ Other: _____

CREATIVITY: ☐ Songwriting ☐ Composition ☐ Improvisation ☐ Listening & Study ☐ Lyrics
☐ Other: _____

PERFORMANCE & PROJECTS: ☐ Recording ☐ Backing Tracks ☐ Group Work ☐ Research
☐ Other: _____

TEACHER / ASSIGNMENTS / IMPROVEMENTS

_____
_____
_____
_____
_____

PROGRESS SNAPSHOT (Circle how today's practice went:)

☹   🙁   😐   🙂   😄

NEXT PRACTICE GOALS

_____
_____
_____

DAILY TIP:

Practice tone very quietly and very loudly.

PRACTICE SESSION

DAY / DATE: _____ INSTRUMENT _____
Motivation: ☐ Low ☐ Medium ☐ High

TODAY'S FOCUS
1. _____
2. _____
3. _____

PRACTICE TIME
Planned: ☐ 10 ☐ 20 ☐ 30 ☐ 45 ☐ 60+ minutes   Actual Practice: _____

WHAT YOU PRACTICED TODAY

PLAYING: ☐ New Music ☐ Repertoire ☐ Excerpt Practice ☐ Riffs & Solos ☐ Improvisation
☐ Other: _____

TECHNIQUE & SKILLS: ☐ Scales ☐ Chords ☐ Arpeggios ☐ Ear Training ☐ Exercises
☐ Rhythm & Reading ☐ Applied Theory ☐ Other: _____

CREATIVITY: ☐ Songwriting ☐ Composition ☐ Improvisation ☐ Listening & Study ☐ Lyrics
☐ Other: _____

PERFORMANCE & PROJECTS: ☐ Recording ☐ Backing Tracks ☐ Group Work ☐ Research
☐ Other: _____

TEACHER / ASSIGNMENTS / IMPROVEMENTS
_____
_____
_____
_____
_____

PROGRESS SNAPSHOT (Circle how today's practice went:)

☹ ☹ 😐 🙂 😄

NEXT PRACTICE GOALS
_____
_____
_____
_____
_____

DAY SESSION

PRACTICE SESSION

DAY / DATE: _____ INSTRUMENT _____
Motivation: ☐ Low ☐ Medium ☐ High

TODAY'S FOCUS

1. _____
2. _____
3. _____

PRACTICE TIME

Planned: ☐ 10 ☐ 20 ☐ 30 ☐ 45 ☐ 60+ minutes   Actual Practice: _____

WHAT YOU PRACTICED TODAY

PLAYING: ☐ New Music ☐ Repertoire ☐ Excerpt Practice ☐ Riffs & Solos ☐ Improvisation
☐ Other: _____

TECHNIQUE & SKILLS: ☐ Scales ☐ Chords ☐ Arpeggios ☐ Ear Training ☐ Exercises
☐ Rhythm & Reading ☐ Applied Theory ☐ Other: _____

CREATIVITY: ☐ Songwriting ☐ Composition ☐ Improvisation ☐ Listening & Study ☐ Lyrics
☐ Other: _____

PERFORMANCE & PROJECTS: ☐ Recording ☐ Backing Tracks ☐ Group Work ☐ Research
☐ Other: _____

TEACHER / ASSIGNMENTS / IMPROVEMENTS

_____
_____
_____
_____
_____

PROGRESS SNAPSHOT (Circle how today's practice went:)

☹   🙁   😐   🙂   😊

NEXT PRACTICE GOALS

_____
_____
_____

DAILY TIP:

The silence between notes holds truth. Mozart

PRACTICE SUMMARY

DATE RANGE: _____
TOTAL SESSIONS: _____ TOTAL TIME: _____

OVERALL FOCUS / ENERGY THIS PERIOD
☐ Strong Momentum ☐ Balanced Progress ☐ Slower Week ☐ Reset / Recovery

TOP 3 ACCOMPLISHMENTS
1. _____
2. _____
3. _____

WHAT YOU WORKED ON MOST
PLAYING: _____
_____

TECHNIQUE & SKILLS: _____
_____

CREATIVITY: _____
_____

PERFORMANCE & PROJECTS: _____
_____

DEEP PRACTICE RECAP
Piece / Exercise: _____
Current Metronome: _____ bpm   Goal: _____ bpm
Focus Area: ☐ Tone ☐ Timing ☐ Fingering ☐ Articulation ☐ Other
Improvement Plan: _____

PERFORMANCES
☐ Recorded / Video ☐ Played for Someone ☐ Ensemble / Jam ☐ None this Week

PROGRESS & INSIGHTS
What improved the most? _____
What still needs work? _____
Creative discoveries or ideas? _____

NEXT FOCUS / UPCOMING GOALS
_____
_____
_____

WEEKLY INSIGHT
Choose one weakness and make it your focus for the next three days.

TEACHER / LESSON NOTES

LESSON DATE: _____ INSTRUMENT _____

Readiness: ☐ Low ☐ Medium ☐ High

ASSIGNMENTS / FOCUS POINTS

1. _____
2. _____
3. _____
4. _____
5. _____

HOW LONG YOU SHOULD PRACTICE AT EACH SESSION

Planned: ☐ 10 ☐ 20 ☐ 30 ☐ 45 ☐ 60+ minutes   Other: _____

TECHNIQUE & SKILLS: ☐ Scales ☐ Chords ☐ Arpeggios ☐ Ear Training ☐ Exercises
☐ Rhythm & Reading ☐ Applied Theory ☐ Other: _____
_____
_____

REPERTOIRE 1
Title / Section: _____
Measures / Focus: _____ Tempo Goal: _____ bpm

REPERTOIRE 2
Title / Section: _____
Measures / Focus: _____ Tempo Goal: _____ bpm

REPERTOIRE 3
Title / Section: _____
Measures / Focus: _____ Tempo Goal: _____ bpm

TEACHER COMMENTS
_____
_____
_____
_____
_____

STUDENT NOTES
_____
_____
_____

IDEAS & NOTES

MONTHLY REFLECTION

MONTH: _____ TOTAL TIME: _____
TOTAL SESSIONS: _____ TOTAL PERFORMANCES: _____

RATE YOUR PROGRESS THIS MONTH: BELOW ★ AVERAGE ★ ★ ABOVE ★ ★ ★

WHAT ARE YOU MOST GRATEFUL FOR WITH YOUR MUSIC THIS MONTH

_____
_____
_____
_____

SET YOUR GOALS FOR NEXT MONTH

_____
_____
_____
_____

POSITIVE LESSONS OR HABITS TO CONTINUE NEXT MONTH

_____
_____
_____
_____

NOTES

_____
_____
_____
_____

INSIGHT

The greatest music is always unfinished, for it lives and breathes anew with every single performance.

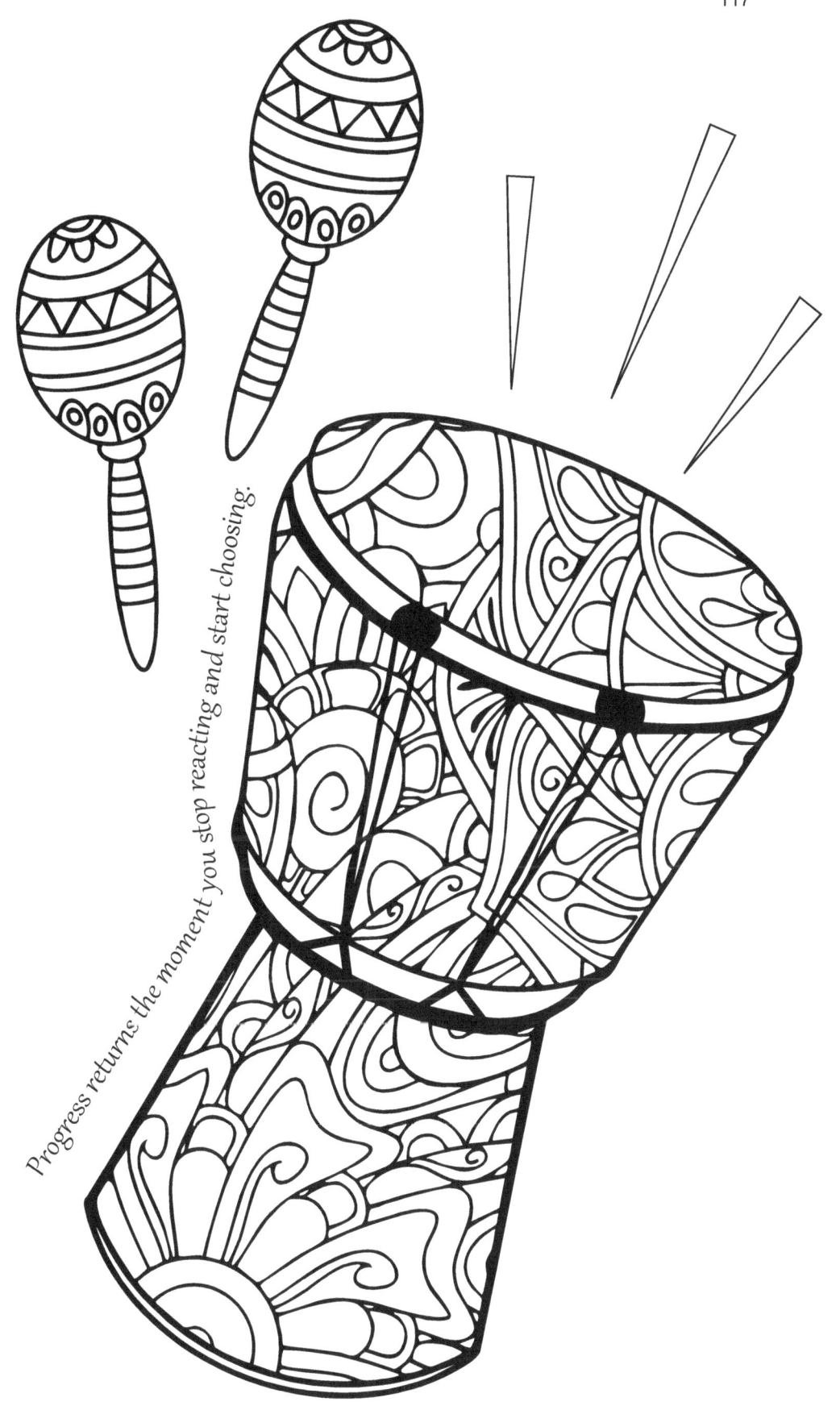

Progress returns the moment you stop reacting and start choosing.

PRACTICE SESSION

DAY / DATE: _____ INSTRUMENT _____
Motivation: ☐ Low ☐ Medium ☐ High

TODAY'S FOCUS

1. _____
2. _____
3. _____

PRACTICE TIME

Planned: ☐ 10 ☐ 20 ☐ 30 ☐ 45 ☐ 60+ minutes   Actual Practice: _____

WHAT YOU PRACTICED TODAY

PLAYING: ☐ New Music ☐ Repertoire ☐ Excerpt Practice ☐ Riffs & Solos ☐ Improvisation
☐ Other: _____

TECHNIQUE & SKILLS: ☐ Scales ☐ Chords ☐ Arpeggios ☐ Ear Training ☐ Exercises
☐ Rhythm & Reading ☐ Applied Theory ☐ Other: _____

CREATIVITY: ☐ Songwriting ☐ Composition ☐ Improvisation ☐ Listening & Study ☐ Lyrics
☐ Other: _____

PERFORMANCE & PROJECTS: ☐ Recording ☐ Backing Tracks ☐ Group Work ☐ Research
☐ Other: _____

TEACHER / ASSIGNMENTS / IMPROVEMENTS

_____
_____
_____
_____
_____

PROGRESS SNAPSHOT (Circle how today's practice went:)

☹ 😕 😐 🙂 😄

NEXT PRACTICE GOALS

_____
_____
_____

DAILY TIP:

Every piece has a perfect tempo.

PRACTICE SESSION

DAY / DATE: _____ INSTRUMENT _____
Motivation: ☐ Low   ☐ Medium   ☐ High

TODAY'S FOCUS
1. _____
2. _____
3. _____

PRACTICE TIME
Planned: ☐ 10 ☐ 20 ☐ 30 ☐ 45 ☐ 60+ minutes   Actual Practice: _____

WHAT YOU PRACTICED TODAY

PLAYING: ☐ New Music ☐ Repertoire ☐ Excerpt Practice ☐ Riffs & Solos ☐ Improvisation
☐ Other: _____

TECHNIQUE & SKILLS: ☐ Scales ☐ Chords ☐ Arpeggios ☐ Ear Training ☐ Exercises
☐ Rhythm & Reading ☐ Applied Theory ☐ Other: _____

CREATIVITY: ☐ Songwriting ☐ Composition ☐ Improvisation ☐ Listening & Study ☐ Lyrics
☐ Other: _____

PERFORMANCE & PROJECTS: ☐ Recording ☐ Backing Tracks ☐ Group Work ☐ Research
☐ Other: _____

TEACHER / ASSIGNMENTS / IMPROVEMENTS
_____
_____
_____
_____
_____

PROGRESS SNAPSHOT (Circle how today's practice went:)

☹   🙁   😐   🙂   😄

NEXT PRACTICE GOALS
_____
_____
_____
_____
_____

PRACTICE SESSION

DAY / DATE: _____ INSTRUMENT _____
Motivation: ☐ Low ☐ Medium ☐ High

TODAY'S FOCUS

1. _____
2. _____
3. _____

PRACTICE TIME

Planned: ☐ 10 ☐ 20 ☐ 30 ☐ 45 ☐ 60+ minutes   Actual Practice: _____

WHAT YOU PRACTICED TODAY

PLAYING: ☐ New Music ☐ Repertoire ☐ Excerpt Practice ☐ Riffs & Solos ☐ Improvisation
☐ Other: _____

TECHNIQUE & SKILLS: ☐ Scales ☐ Chords ☐ Arpeggios ☐ Ear Training ☐ Exercises
☐ Rhythm & Reading ☐ Applied Theory ☐ Other: _____
_____

CREATIVITY: ☐ Songwriting ☐ Composition ☐ Improvisation ☐ Listening & Study ☐ Lyrics
☐ Other: _____

PERFORMANCE & PROJECTS: ☐ Recording ☐ Backing Tracks ☐ Group Work ☐ Research
☐ Other: _____

TEACHER / ASSIGNMENTS / IMPROVEMENTS

_____
_____
_____
_____
_____

PROGRESS SNAPSHOT (Circle how today's practice went:)

😠 ☹ 😐 🙂 😄

NEXT PRACTICE GOALS

_____
_____
_____

DAILY TIP:

Play for yourself first. Liszt.

PRACTICE SESSION

DAY / DATE: _____ INSTRUMENT _____
Motivation: ☐ Low ☐ Medium ☐ High

TODAY'S FOCUS
1. _____
2. _____
3. _____

PRACTICE TIME
Planned: ☐ 10 ☐ 20 ☐ 30 ☐ 45 ☐ 60+ minutes   Actual Practice: _____

WHAT YOU PRACTICED TODAY

PLAYING: ☐ New Music ☐ Repertoire ☐ Excerpt Practice ☐ Riffs & Solos ☐ Improvisation
☐ Other: _____

TECHNIQUE & SKILLS: ☐ Scales ☐ Chords ☐ Arpeggios ☐ Ear Training ☐ Exercises
☐ Rhythm & Reading ☐ Applied Theory ☐ Other: _____

CREATIVITY: ☐ Songwriting ☐ Composition ☐ Improvisation ☐ Listening & Study ☐ Lyrics
☐ Other: _____

PERFORMANCE & PROJECTS: ☐ Recording ☐ Backing Tracks ☐ Group Work ☐ Research
☐ Other: _____

TEACHER / ASSIGNMENTS / IMPROVEMENTS
_____
_____
_____
_____
_____

PROGRESS SNAPSHOT (Circle how today's practice went:)

😠   🙁   😐   🙂   😄

NEXT PRACTICE GOALS
_____
_____
_____
_____
_____

PRACTICE SESSION

DAY / DATE: _____ INSTRUMENT _____
Motivation: ☐ Low   ☐ Medium   ☐ High

TODAY'S FOCUS

1. _____
2. _____
3. _____

PRACTICE TIME

Planned: ☐ 10   ☐ 20   ☐ 30   ☐ 45   ☐ 60+ minutes   Actual Practice: _____

WHAT YOU PRACTICED TODAY

PLAYING: ☐ New Music ☐ Repertoire ☐ Excerpt Practice ☐ Riffs & Solos ☐ Improvisation
☐ Other: _____

TECHNIQUE & SKILLS: ☐ Scales ☐ Chords ☐ Arpeggios ☐ Ear Training ☐ Exercises
☐ Rhythm & Reading ☐ Applied Theory ☐ Other: _____

CREATIVITY: ☐ Songwriting ☐ Composition ☐ Improvisation ☐ Listening & Study ☐ Lyrics
☐ Other: _____

PERFORMANCE & PROJECTS: ☐ Recording ☐ Backing Tracks ☐ Group Work ☐ Research
☐ Other: _____

TEACHER / ASSIGNMENTS / IMPROVEMENTS

_____
_____
_____
_____
_____

PROGRESS SNAPSHOT (Circle how today's practice went:)

😠   ☹   😐   🙂   😄

NEXT PRACTICE GOALS

_____
_____
_____

DAILY TIP:

Simplicity is organized complexity. Schoenberg.

PRACTICE SUMMARY

DATE RANGE: _____
TOTAL SESSIONS: _____ TOTAL TIME: _____

OVERALL FOCUS / ENERGY THIS PERIOD
☐ Strong Momentum ☐ Balanced Progress ☐ Slower Week ☐ Reset / Recovery

TOP 3 ACCOMPLISHMENTS
1. _____
2. _____
3. _____

WHAT YOU WORKED ON MOST
PLAYING: _____
_____

TECHNIQUE & SKILLS: _____
_____

CREATIVITY: _____
_____

PERFORMANCE & PROJECTS: _____
_____

DEEP PRACTICE RECAP
Piece / Exercise: _____
Current Metronome: _____ bpm   Goal: _____ bpm
Focus Area: ☐ Tone ☐ Timing ☐ Fingering ☐ Articulation ☐ Other
Improvement Plan: _____

PERFORMANCES
☐ Recorded / Video ☐ Played for Someone ☐ Ensemble /Jam ☐ None this Week

PROGRESS & INSIGHTS
What improved the most? _____
What still needs work? _____
Creative discoveries or ideas? _____

NEXT FOCUS / UPCOMING GOALS
_____
_____
_____

WEEKLY INSIGHT
Identify the patterns that repeat in your mistakes; they are your real teachers.

WEEK SUMMARY

PRACTICE SESSION

DAY / DATE: _____   INSTRUMENT _____

Motivation: ☐ Low   ☐ Medium   ☐ High

TODAY'S FOCUS

1. _____

2. _____

3. _____

PRACTICE TIME

Planned: ☐ 10   ☐ 20   ☐ 30   ☐ 45   ☐ 60+ minutes   Actual Practice: _____

WHAT YOU PRACTICED TODAY

PLAYING: ☐ New Music ☐ Repertoire ☐ Excerpt Practice ☐ Riffs & Solos ☐ Improvisation
☐ Other: _____

TECHNIQUE & SKILLS: ☐ Scales ☐ Chords ☐ Arpeggios ☐ Ear Training ☐ Exercises
☐ Rhythm & Reading ☐ Applied Theory ☐ Other: _____
_____

CREATIVITY: ☐ Songwriting ☐ Composition ☐ Improvisation ☐ Listening & Study ☐ Lyrics
☐ Other: _____

PERFORMANCE & PROJECTS: ☐ Recording ☐ Backing Tracks ☐ Group Work ☐ Research
☐ Other: _____

TEACHER / ASSIGNMENTS / IMPROVEMENTS

_____

_____

_____

_____

_____

PROGRESS SNAPSHOT (Circle how today's practice went:)

☹   🙁   😐   🙂   😄

NEXT PRACTICE GOALS

_____

_____

_____

DAILY TIP:

Treat the metronome like another instrument, not a master.

PRACTICE SESSION

DAY / DATE: _____ INSTRUMENT _____

Motivation: ☐ Low   ☐ Medium   ☐ High

TODAY'S FOCUS
1. _____
2. _____
3. _____

PRACTICE TIME
Planned: ☐ 10 ☐ 20 ☐ 30 ☐ 45 ☐ 60+ minutes   Actual Practice: _____

WHAT YOU PRACTICED TODAY

PLAYING: ☐ New Music ☐ Repertoire ☐ Excerpt Practice ☐ Riffs & Solos ☐ Improvisation
☐ Other: _____

TECHNIQUE & SKILLS: ☐ Scales ☐ Chords ☐ Arpeggios ☐ Ear Training ☐ Exercises
☐ Rhythm & Reading ☐ Applied Theory ☐ Other: _____

CREATIVITY: ☐ Songwriting ☐ Composition ☐ Improvisation ☐ Listening & Study ☐ Lyrics
☐ Other: _____

PERFORMANCE & PROJECTS: ☐ Recording ☐ Backing Tracks ☐ Group Work ☐ Research
☐ Other: _____

TEACHER / ASSIGNMENTS / IMPROVEMENTS
_____
_____
_____
_____
_____

PROGRESS SNAPSHOT (Circle how today's practice went:)

😠   😕   😐   🙂   😄

NEXT PRACTICE GOALS
_____
_____
_____
_____
_____

PRACTICE SESSION

DAY / DATE: _____ INSTRUMENT _____
Motivation: ☐ Low ☐ Medium ☐ High

TODAY'S FOCUS
1. _____
2. _____
3. _____

PRACTICE TIME
Planned: ☐ 10 ☐ 20 ☐ 30 ☐ 45 ☐ 60+ minutes   Actual Practice: _____

WHAT YOU PRACTICED TODAY

PLAYING: ☐ New Music ☐ Repertoire ☐ Excerpt Practice ☐ Riffs & Solos ☐ Improvisation
☐ Other: _____

TECHNIQUE & SKILLS: ☐ Scales ☐ Chords ☐ Arpeggios ☐ Ear Training ☐ Exercises
☐ Rhythm & Reading ☐ Applied Theory ☐ Other: _____

CREATIVITY: ☐ Songwriting ☐ Composition ☐ Improvisation ☐ Listening & Study ☐ Lyrics
☐ Other: _____

PERFORMANCE & PROJECTS: ☐ Recording ☐ Backing Tracks ☐ Group Work ☐ Research
☐ Other: _____

TEACHER / ASSIGNMENTS / IMPROVEMENTS
_____
_____
_____
_____
_____

PROGRESS SNAPSHOT (Circle how today's practice went:)
☹ ☹ 😐 🙂 😄

NEXT PRACTICE GOALS
_____
_____
_____

DAILY TIP:
Work backwards through difficult passages.

PRACTICE SESSION

DAY / DATE: _____ INSTRUMENT _____
Motivation: ☐ Low ☐ Medium ☐ High

TODAY'S FOCUS

1. _____
2. _____
3. _____

PRACTICE TIME

Planned: ☐ 10 ☐ 20 ☐ 30 ☐ 45 ☐ 60+ minutes   Actual Practice: _____

WHAT YOU PRACTICED TODAY

PLAYING: ☐ New Music ☐ Repertoire ☐ Excerpt Practice ☐ Riffs & Solos ☐ Improvisation
☐ Other: _____

TECHNIQUE & SKILLS: ☐ Scales ☐ Chords ☐ Arpeggios ☐ Ear Training ☐ Exercises
☐ Rhythm & Reading ☐ Applied Theory ☐ Other: _____

CREATIVITY: ☐ Songwriting ☐ Composition ☐ Improvisation ☐ Listening & Study ☐ Lyrics
☐ Other: _____

PERFORMANCE & PROJECTS: ☐ Recording ☐ Backing Tracks ☐ Group Work ☐ Research
☐ Other: _____

TEACHER / ASSIGNMENTS / IMPROVEMENTS

_____
_____
_____
_____
_____

PROGRESS SNAPSHOT (Circle how today's practice went:)

☹ 🙁 😐 🙂 😊

NEXT PRACTICE GOALS

_____
_____
_____
_____
_____

PRACTICE SESSION

DAY / DATE: _____   INSTRUMENT _____
Motivation: ☐ Low   ☐ Medium   ☐ High

TODAY'S FOCUS

1. _____
2. _____
3. _____

PRACTICE TIME

Planned: ☐ 10   ☐ 20   ☐ 30   ☐ 45   ☐ 60+ minutes   Actual Practice: _____

WHAT YOU PRACTICED TODAY

PLAYING: ☐ New Music ☐ Repertoire ☐ Excerpt Practice ☐ Riffs & Solos ☐ Improvisation
☐ Other: _____

TECHNIQUE & SKILLS: ☐ Scales ☐ Chords ☐ Arpeggios ☐ Ear Training ☐ Exercises
☐ Rhythm & Reading ☐ Applied Theory ☐ Other: _____

CREATIVITY: ☐ Songwriting ☐ Composition ☐ Improvisation ☐ Listening & Study ☐ Lyrics
☐ Other: _____

PERFORMANCE & PROJECTS: ☐ Recording ☐ Backing Tracks ☐ Group Work ☐ Research
☐ Other: _____

TEACHER / ASSIGNMENTS / IMPROVEMENTS

_____
_____
_____
_____
_____

PROGRESS SNAPSHOT (Circle how today's practice went:)

😠   🙁   😐   🙂   😄

NEXT PRACTICE GOALS

_____
_____
_____

DAILY TIP:

Practice endings more than beginnings.

PRACTICE SUMMARY

DATE RANGE: _____
TOTAL SESSIONS: _____ TOTAL TIME: _____

OVERALL FOCUS / ENERGY THIS PERIOD
☐ Strong Momentum ☐ Balanced Progress ☐ Slower Week ☐ Reset / Recovery

TOP 3 ACCOMPLISHMENTS
1. _____
2. _____
3. _____

WHAT YOU WORKED ON MOST

PLAYING: _____
_____

TECHNIQUE & SKILLS: _____
_____

CREATIVITY: _____
_____

PERFORMANCE & PROJECTS: _____
_____

DEEP PRACTICE RECAP
Piece / Exercise: _____
Current Metronome: _____ bpm   Goal: _____ bpm
Focus Area: ☐ Tone ☐ Timing ☐ Fingering ☐ Articulation ☐ Other
Improvement Plan: _____

PERFORMANCES
☐ Recorded / Video ☐ Played for Someone ☐ Ensemble /Jam ☐ None this Week

PROGRESS & INSIGHTS
What improved the most? _____
What still needs work? _____
Creative discoveries or ideas? _____

NEXT FOCUS / UPCOMING GOALS
_____
_____
_____

WEEKLY INSIGHT
Ask yourself what you avoided practicing this week and face it next.

WEEK SUMMARY

TEACHER / LESSON NOTES

LESSON DATE: _____ INSTRUMENT _____
Readiness: ☐ Low   ☐ Medium   ☐ High

ASSIGNMENTS / FOCUS POINTS

1. _____
2. _____
3. _____
4. _____
5. _____

HOW LONG YOU SHOULD PRACTICE AT EACH SESSION

Planned: ☐ 10   ☐ 20   ☐ 30   ☐ 45   ☐ 60+ minutes   Other: _____

TECHNIQUE & SKILLS: ☐ Scales   ☐ Chords   ☐ Arpeggios   ☐ Ear Training   ☐ Exercises
☐ Rhythm & Reading   ☐ Applied Theory   ☐ Other: _____
_____
_____

REPERTOIRE 1
Title / Section: _____
Measures / Focus: _____ Tempo Goal: _____ bpm

REPERTOIRE 2
Title / Section: _____
Measures / Focus: _____ Tempo Goal: _____ bpm

REPERTOIRE 3
Title / Section: _____
Measures / Focus: _____ Tempo Goal: _____ bpm

TEACHER COMMENTS
_____
_____
_____
_____
_____

STUDENT NOTES
_____
_____
_____

IDEAS & NOTES

PRACTICE SESSION

DAY / DATE: _____ INSTRUMENT _____

Motivation: ☐ Low ☐ Medium ☐ High

TODAY'S FOCUS

1. _____
2. _____
3. _____

PRACTICE TIME

Planned: ☐ 10 ☐ 20 ☐ 30 ☐ 45 ☐ 60+ minutes   Actual Practice: _____

WHAT YOU PRACTICED TODAY

PLAYING: ☐ New Music ☐ Repertoire ☐ Excerpt Practice ☐ Riffs & Solos ☐ Improvisation
☐ Other: _____

TECHNIQUE & SKILLS: ☐ Scales ☐ Chords ☐ Arpeggios ☐ Ear Training ☐ Exercises
☐ Rhythm & Reading ☐ Applied Theory ☐ Other: _____

CREATIVITY: ☐ Songwriting ☐ Composition ☐ Improvisation ☐ Listening & Study ☐ Lyrics
☐ Other: _____

PERFORMANCE & PROJECTS: ☐ Recording ☐ Backing Tracks ☐ Group Work ☐ Research
☐ Other: _____

TEACHER / ASSIGNMENTS / IMPROVEMENTS

_____
_____
_____
_____
_____

PROGRESS SNAPSHOT (Circle how today's practice went:)

☹ ☹ 😐 🙂 😊

NEXT PRACTICE GOALS

_____
_____
_____

DAILY TIP:

Transpose an simple tune into a new key daily.

PRACTICE SESSION

DAY / DATE: _____ INSTRUMENT _____
Motivation: ☐ Low ☐ Medium ☐ High

TODAY'S FOCUS
1. _____
2. _____
3. _____

PRACTICE TIME
Planned: ☐ 10 ☐ 20 ☐ 30 ☐ 45 ☐ 60+ minutes   Actual Practice: _____

WHAT YOU PRACTICED TODAY

PLAYING: ☐ New Music ☐ Repertoire ☐ Excerpt Practice ☐ Riffs & Solos ☐ Improvisation
☐ Other: _____

TECHNIQUE & SKILLS: ☐ Scales ☐ Chords ☐ Arpeggios ☐ Ear Training ☐ Exercises
☐ Rhythm & Reading ☐ Applied Theory ☐ Other: _____

CREATIVITY: ☐ Songwriting ☐ Composition ☐ Improvisation ☐ Listening & Study ☐ Lyrics
☐ Other: _____

PERFORMANCE & PROJECTS: ☐ Recording ☐ Backing Tracks ☐ Group Work ☐ Research
☐ Other: _____

TEACHER / ASSIGNMENTS / IMPROVEMENTS
_____
_____
_____
_____
_____

PROGRESS SNAPSHOT (Circle how today's practice went:)

😠   🙁   😐   🙂   😄

NEXT PRACTICE GOALS
_____
_____
_____
_____
_____

DAY SESSION

PRACTICE SESSION

DAY / DATE: _____ INSTRUMENT _____
Motivation: ☐ Low ☐ Medium ☐ High

TODAY'S FOCUS

1. _____
2. _____
3. _____

PRACTICE TIME

Planned: ☐ 10 ☐ 20 ☐ 30 ☐ 45 ☐ 60+ minutes   Actual Practice: _____

WHAT YOU PRACTICED TODAY

PLAYING: ☐ New Music ☐ Repertoire ☐ Excerpt Practice ☐ Riffs & Solos ☐ Improvisation
☐ Other: _____

TECHNIQUE & SKILLS: ☐ Scales ☐ Chords ☐ Arpeggios ☐ Ear Training ☐ Exercises
☐ Rhythm & Reading ☐ Applied Theory ☐ Other: _____

CREATIVITY: ☐ Songwriting ☐ Composition ☐ Improvisation ☐ Listening & Study ☐ Lyrics
☐ Other: _____

PERFORMANCE & PROJECTS: ☐ Recording ☐ Backing Tracks ☐ Group Work ☐ Research
☐ Other: _____

TEACHER / ASSIGNMENTS / IMPROVEMENTS

_____
_____
_____
_____
_____

PROGRESS SNAPSHOT (Circle how today's practice went:)

☹ 🙁 😐 🙂 😄

NEXT PRACTICE GOALS

_____
_____
_____

DAILY TIP:

Transpose a familiar melody from major to minor.

PRACTICE SESSION

DAY / DATE: _____ INSTRUMENT _____

Motivation: ☐ Low ☐ Medium ☐ High

TODAY'S FOCUS

1. _____
2. _____
3. _____

PRACTICE TIME

Planned: ☐ 10 ☐ 20 ☐ 30 ☐ 45 ☐ 60+ minutes   Actual Practice: _____

WHAT YOU PRACTICED TODAY

PLAYING: ☐ New Music ☐ Repertoire ☐ Excerpt Practice ☐ Riffs & Solos ☐ Improvisation
☐ Other: _____

TECHNIQUE & SKILLS: ☐ Scales ☐ Chords ☐ Arpeggios ☐ Ear Training ☐ Exercises
☐ Rhythm & Reading ☐ Applied Theory ☐ Other: _____

CREATIVITY: ☐ Songwriting ☐ Composition ☐ Improvisation ☐ Listening & Study ☐ Lyrics
☐ Other: _____

PERFORMANCE & PROJECTS: ☐ Recording ☐ Backing Tracks ☐ Group Work ☐ Research
☐ Other: _____

TEACHER / ASSIGNMENTS / IMPROVEMENTS

_____
_____
_____
_____
_____

PROGRESS SNAPSHOT (Circle how today's practice went:)

☹ 🙁 😐 🙂 😃

NEXT PRACTICE GOALS

_____
_____
_____
_____
_____

DAY SESSION

PRACTICE SESSION

DAY / DATE: _____ INSTRUMENT _____
Motivation: ☐ Low ☐ Medium ☐ High

TODAY'S FOCUS

1. _____
2. _____
3. _____

PRACTICE TIME

Planned: ☐ 10 ☐ 20 ☐ 30 ☐ 45 ☐ 60+ minutes   Actual Practice: _____

WHAT YOU PRACTICED TODAY

PLAYING: ☐ New Music ☐ Repertoire ☐ Excerpt Practice ☐ Riffs & Solos ☐ Improvisation
☐ Other: _____

TECHNIQUE & SKILLS: ☐ Scales ☐ Chords ☐ Arpeggios ☐ Ear Training ☐ Exercises
☐ Rhythm & Reading ☐ Applied Theory ☐ Other: _____

CREATIVITY: ☐ Songwriting ☐ Composition ☐ Improvisation ☐ Listening & Study ☐ Lyrics
☐ Other: _____

PERFORMANCE & PROJECTS: ☐ Recording ☐ Backing Tracks ☐ Group Work ☐ Research
☐ Other: _____

TEACHER / ASSIGNMENTS / IMPROVEMENTS

_____
_____
_____
_____
_____

PROGRESS SNAPSHOT (Circle how today's practice went:)

☹ 🙁 😐 🙂 😄

NEXT PRACTICE GOALS

_____
_____
_____

DAILY TIP:

Don't rush the rest.

PRACTICE SUMMARY

DATE RANGE: _____
TOTAL SESSIONS: _____ TOTAL TIME: _____

OVERALL FOCUS / ENERGY THIS PERIOD
☐ Strong Momentum ☐ Balanced Progress ☐ Slower Week ☐ Reset / Recovery

TOP 3 ACCOMPLISHMENTS
1. _____
2. _____
3. _____

WHAT YOU WORKED ON MOST

PLAYING: _____
_____

TECHNIQUE & SKILLS: _____
_____

CREATIVITY: _____
_____

PERFORMANCE & PROJECTS: _____
_____

DEEP PRACTICE RECAP
Piece / Exercise: _____
Current Metronome: _____ bpm   Goal: _____ bpm
Focus Area: ☐ Tone ☐ Timing ☐ Fingering ☐ Articulation ☐ Other
Improvement Plan: _____

PERFORMANCES
☐ Recorded / Video ☐ Played for Someone ☐ Ensemble / Jam ☐ None this Week

PROGRESS & INSIGHTS
What improved the most? _____
What still needs work? _____
Creative discoveries or ideas? _____

NEXT FOCUS / UPCOMING GOALS
_____
_____
_____

WEEKLY INSIGHT
Trade speed for clarity and listen for the spaces between notes.

PRACTICE SESSION

DAY / DATE: _____ INSTRUMENT _____
Motivation: ☐ Low ☐ Medium ☐ High

TODAY'S FOCUS

1. _____
2. _____
3. _____

PRACTICE TIME

Planned: ☐ 10 ☐ 20 ☐ 30 ☐ 45 ☐ 60+ minutes   Actual Practice: _____

WHAT YOU PRACTICED TODAY

PLAYING: ☐ New Music ☐ Repertoire ☐ Excerpt Practice ☐ Riffs & Solos ☐ Improvisation
☐ Other: _____

TECHNIQUE & SKILLS: ☐ Scales ☐ Chords ☐ Arpeggios ☐ Ear Training ☐ Exercises
☐ Rhythm & Reading ☐ Applied Theory ☐ Other: _____

CREATIVITY: ☐ Songwriting ☐ Composition ☐ Improvisation ☐ Listening & Study ☐ Lyrics
☐ Other: _____

PERFORMANCE & PROJECTS: ☐ Recording ☐ Backing Tracks ☐ Group Work ☐ Research
☐ Other: _____

TEACHER / ASSIGNMENTS / IMPROVEMENTS

_____
_____
_____
_____
_____

PROGRESS SNAPSHOT (Circle how today's practice went:)

☹ 🙁 😐 🙂 😊

NEXT PRACTICE GOALS

_____
_____
_____

DAILY TIP:

Thoughtful practice and meditation produce the similar results.

PRACTICE SESSION

DAY / DATE: _____ INSTRUMENT _____

Motivation: ☐ Low ☐ Medium ☐ High

TODAY'S FOCUS

1. _____
2. _____
3. _____

PRACTICE TIME

Planned: ☐ 10 ☐ 20 ☐ 30 ☐ 45 ☐ 60+ minutes   Actual Practice: _____

WHAT YOU PRACTICED TODAY

PLAYING: ☐ New Music ☐ Repertoire ☐ Excerpt Practice ☐ Riffs & Solos ☐ Improvisation
☐ Other: _____

TECHNIQUE & SKILLS: ☐ Scales ☐ Chords ☐ Arpeggios ☐ Ear Training ☐ Exercises
☐ Rhythm & Reading ☐ Applied Theory ☐ Other: _____
_____

CREATIVITY: ☐ Songwriting ☐ Composition ☐ Improvisation ☐ Listening & Study ☐ Lyrics
☐ Other: _____

PERFORMANCE & PROJECTS: ☐ Recording ☐ Backing Tracks ☐ Group Work ☐ Research
☐ Other: _____

TEACHER / ASSIGNMENTS / IMPROVEMENTS

_____
_____
_____
_____
_____

PROGRESS SNAPSHOT (Circle how today's practice went:)

☹ 🙁 😐 🙂 😄

NEXT PRACTICE GOALS

_____
_____
_____
_____
_____

PRACTICE SESSION

DAY / DATE: _____   INSTRUMENT _____
Motivation: ☐ Low   ☐ Medium   ☐ High

TODAY'S FOCUS

1. _____
2. _____
3. _____

PRACTICE TIME

Planned: ☐ 10   ☐ 20   ☐ 30   ☐ 45   ☐ 60+ minutes   Actual Practice: _____

WHAT YOU PRACTICED TODAY

PLAYING: ☐ New Music ☐ Repertoire ☐ Excerpt Practice ☐ Riffs & Solos ☐ Improvisation
☐ Other: _____

TECHNIQUE & SKILLS: ☐ Scales ☐ Chords ☐ Arpeggios ☐ Ear Training ☐ Exercises
☐ Rhythm & Reading ☐ Applied Theory ☐ Other: _____
_____

CREATIVITY: ☐ Songwriting ☐ Composition ☐ Improvisation ☐ Listening & Study ☐ Lyrics
☐ Other: _____

PERFORMANCE & PROJECTS: ☐ Recording ☐ Backing Tracks ☐ Group Work ☐ Research
☐ Other: _____

TEACHER / ASSIGNMENTS / IMPROVEMENTS

_____
_____
_____
_____
_____

PROGRESS SNAPSHOT (Circle how today's practice went:)

☹   🙁   😐   🙂   😊

NEXT PRACTICE GOALS

_____
_____
_____

DAILY TIP:

The listener's soul is your first concern. Schumann

PRACTICE SESSION

DAY / DATE: _____ INSTRUMENT _____
Motivation: ☐ Low ☐ Medium ☐ High

TODAY'S FOCUS
1. _____
2. _____
3. _____

PRACTICE TIME
Planned: ☐ 10 ☐ 20 ☐ 30 ☐ 45 ☐ 60+ minutes   Actual Practice: _____

WHAT YOU PRACTICED TODAY

PLAYING: ☐ New Music ☐ Repertoire ☐ Excerpt Practice ☐ Riffs & Solos ☐ Improvisation
☐ Other: _____

TECHNIQUE & SKILLS: ☐ Scales ☐ Chords ☐ Arpeggios ☐ Ear Training ☐ Exercises
☐ Rhythm & Reading ☐ Applied Theory ☐ Other: _____

CREATIVITY: ☐ Songwriting ☐ Composition ☐ Improvisation ☐ Listening & Study ☐ Lyrics
☐ Other: _____

PERFORMANCE & PROJECTS: ☐ Recording ☐ Backing Tracks ☐ Group Work ☐ Research
☐ Other: _____

TEACHER / ASSIGNMENTS / IMPROVEMENTS
_____
_____
_____
_____
_____

PROGRESS SNAPSHOT (Circle how today's practice went:)

😠   🙁   😐   🙂   😄

NEXT PRACTICE GOALS
_____
_____
_____
_____
_____

DAY SESSION

PRACTICE SESSION

DAY / DATE: _____ INSTRUMENT _____

Motivation: ☐ Low ☐ Medium ☐ High

TODAY'S FOCUS

1. _____
2. _____
3. _____

PRACTICE TIME

Planned: ☐ 10 ☐ 20 ☐ 30 ☐ 45 ☐ 60+ minutes   Actual Practice: _____

WHAT YOU PRACTICED TODAY

PLAYING: ☐ New Music ☐ Repertoire ☐ Excerpt Practice ☐ Riffs & Solos ☐ Improvisation
☐ Other: _____

TECHNIQUE & SKILLS: ☐ Scales ☐ Chords ☐ Arpeggios ☐ Ear Training ☐ Exercises
☐ Rhythm & Reading ☐ Applied Theory ☐ Other: _____

CREATIVITY: ☐ Songwriting ☐ Composition ☐ Improvisation ☐ Listening & Study ☐ Lyrics
☐ Other: _____

PERFORMANCE & PROJECTS: ☐ Recording ☐ Backing Tracks ☐ Group Work ☐ Research
☐ Other: _____

TEACHER / ASSIGNMENTS / IMPROVEMENTS

_____
_____
_____
_____
_____

PROGRESS SNAPSHOT (Circle how today's practice went:)

☹ 🙁 😐 🙂 😀

NEXT PRACTICE GOALS

_____
_____
_____

DAILY TIP:

Play as if alone, even on stage. Liszt

PRACTICE SUMMARY

DATE RANGE: _____

TOTAL SESSIONS: _____ TOTAL TIME: _____

OVERALL FOCUS / ENERGY THIS PERIOD
☐ Strong Momentum ☐ Balanced Progress ☐ Slower Week ☐ Reset / Recovery

TOP 3 ACCOMPLISHMENTS
1. _____
2. _____
3. _____

WHAT YOU WORKED ON MOST
PLAYING: _____
_____

TECHNIQUE & SKILLS: _____
_____

CREATIVITY: _____
_____

PERFORMANCE & PROJECTS: _____
_____

DEEP PRACTICE RECAP
Piece / Exercise: _____
Current Metronome: _____ bpm   Goal: _____ bpm
Focus Area: ☐ Tone ☐ Timing ☐ Fingering ☐ Articulation ☐ Other
Improvement Plan: _____

PERFORMANCES
☐ Recorded / Video ☐ Played for Someone ☐ Ensemble /Jam ☐ None this Week

PROGRESS & INSIGHTS
What improved the most? _____
What still needs work? _____
Creative discoveries or ideas? _____

NEXT FOCUS / UPCOMING GOALS
_____
_____
_____

WEEKLY INSIGHT
Which practice habit created the most resistance for you this week?
What simple change can you make to eliminate it?

WEEK SUMMARY

TEACHER / LESSON NOTES

LESSON DATE: _____ INSTRUMENT _____
Readiness: ☐ Low ☐ Medium ☐ High

ASSIGNMENTS / FOCUS POINTS

1. _____
2. _____
3. _____
4. _____
5. _____

HOW LONG YOU SHOULD PRACTICE AT EACH SESSION

Planned: ☐ 10 ☐ 20 ☐ 30 ☐ 45 ☐ 60+ minutes Other: _____

TECHNIQUE & SKILLS: ☐ Scales ☐ Chords ☐ Arpeggios ☐ Ear Training ☐ Exercises
☐ Rhythm & Reading ☐ Applied Theory ☐ Other: _____
_____
_____

REPERTOIRE 1
Title / Section: _____
Measures / Focus: _____ Tempo Goal: _____ bpm

REPERTOIRE 2
Title / Section: _____
Measures / Focus: _____ Tempo Goal: _____ bpm

REPERTOIRE 3
Title / Section: _____
Measures / Focus: _____ Tempo Goal: _____ bpm

TEACHER COMMENTS
_____
_____
_____
_____
_____

STUDENT NOTES
_____
_____
_____

IDEAS & NOTES

MONTHLY REFLECTION

MONTH: _____ TOTAL TIME: _____
TOTAL SESSIONS: _____ TOTAL PERFORMANCES: _____

RATE YOUR PROGRESS THIS MONTH: BELOW ★ AVERAGE ★ ★ ABOVE ★ ★ ★

WHAT ARE YOU MOST GRATEFUL FOR WITH YOUR MUSIC THIS MONTH

_____
_____
_____
_____
_____

SET YOUR GOALS FOR NEXT MONTH

_____
_____
_____
_____
_____

POSITIVE LESSONS OR HABITS TO CONTINUE NEXT MONTH

_____
_____
_____
_____
_____

NOTES

_____
_____
_____
_____
_____

INSIGHT

Mastery is the slow deletion of things that do not belong in the music.

PRACTICE SESSION

DAY / DATE: _____ INSTRUMENT _____
Motivation: ☐ Low ☐ Medium ☐ High

TODAY'S FOCUS

1. _____
2. _____
3. _____

PRACTICE TIME

Planned: ☐ 10 ☐ 20 ☐ 30 ☐ 45 ☐ 60+ minutes   Actual Practice: _____

WHAT YOU PRACTICED TODAY

PLAYING: ☐ New Music ☐ Repertoire ☐ Excerpt Practice ☐ Riffs & Solos ☐ Improvisation
☐ Other: _____

TECHNIQUE & SKILLS: ☐ Scales ☐ Chords ☐ Arpeggios ☐ Ear Training ☐ Exercises
☐ Rhythm & Reading ☐ Applied Theory ☐ Other: _____

CREATIVITY: ☐ Songwriting ☐ Composition ☐ Improvisation ☐ Listening & Study ☐ Lyrics
☐ Other: _____

PERFORMANCE & PROJECTS: ☐ Recording ☐ Backing Tracks ☐ Group Work ☐ Research
☐ Other: _____

TEACHER / ASSIGNMENTS / IMPROVEMENTS

_____
_____
_____
_____
_____

PROGRESS SNAPSHOT (Circle how today's practice went:)

☹ 🙁 😐 🙂 😄

NEXT PRACTICE GOALS

_____
_____
_____

DAILY TIP:

Mentally practice away from your instrument every day.

PRACTICE SESSION

DAY / DATE: _____ INSTRUMENT _____
Motivation: ☐ Low ☐ Medium ☐ High

TODAY'S FOCUS
1. _____
2. _____
3. _____

PRACTICE TIME
Planned: ☐ 10 ☐ 20 ☐ 30 ☐ 45 ☐ 60+ minutes   Actual Practice: _____

WHAT YOU PRACTICED TODAY

PLAYING: ☐ New Music ☐ Repertoire ☐ Excerpt Practice ☐ Riffs & Solos ☐ Improvisation
☐ Other: _____

TECHNIQUE & SKILLS: ☐ Scales ☐ Chords ☐ Arpeggios ☐ Ear Training ☐ Exercises
☐ Rhythm & Reading ☐ Applied Theory ☐ Other: _____

CREATIVITY: ☐ Songwriting ☐ Composition ☐ Improvisation ☐ Listening & Study ☐ Lyrics
☐ Other: _____

PERFORMANCE & PROJECTS: ☐ Recording ☐ Backing Tracks ☐ Group Work ☐ Research
☐ Other: _____

TEACHER / ASSIGNMENTS / IMPROVEMENTS

_____
_____
_____
_____
_____

PROGRESS SNAPSHOT (Circle how today's practice went:)

☹   🙁   😐   🙂   😃

NEXT PRACTICE GOALS

_____
_____
_____
_____
_____

PRACTICE SESSION

DAY / DATE: _____ INSTRUMENT _____
Motivation: ☐ Low   ☐ Medium   ☐ High

TODAY'S FOCUS

1. _____
2. _____
3. _____

PRACTICE TIME

Planned: ☐ 10 ☐ 20 ☐ 30 ☐ 45 ☐ 60+ minutes   Actual Practice: _____

WHAT YOU PRACTICED TODAY

PLAYING: ☐ New Music ☐ Repertoire ☐ Excerpt Practice ☐ Riffs & Solos ☐ Improvisation
☐ Other: _____

TECHNIQUE & SKILLS: ☐ Scales ☐ Chords ☐ Arpeggios ☐ Ear Training ☐ Exercises
☐ Rhythm & Reading ☐ Applied Theory ☐ Other: _____

CREATIVITY: ☐ Songwriting ☐ Composition ☐ Improvisation ☐ Listening & Study ☐ Lyrics
☐ Other: _____

PERFORMANCE & PROJECTS: ☐ Recording ☐ Backing Tracks ☐ Group Work ☐ Research
☐ Other: _____

TEACHER / ASSIGNMENTS / IMPROVEMENTS

_____
_____
_____
_____
_____

PROGRESS SNAPSHOT (Circle how today's practice went:)

☹   🙁   😐   🙂   😄

NEXT PRACTICE GOALS

_____
_____
_____

DAILY TIP:

Music survives on tension and release; listen for both.

PRACTICE SESSION

DAY / DATE: _____ INSTRUMENT _____
Motivation: ☐ Low ☐ Medium ☐ High

TODAY'S FOCUS

1. _____
2. _____
3. _____

PRACTICE TIME

Planned: ☐ 10 ☐ 20 ☐ 30 ☐ 45 ☐ 60+ minutes   Actual Practice: _____

WHAT YOU PRACTICED TODAY

PLAYING: ☐ New Music ☐ Repertoire ☐ Excerpt Practice ☐ Riffs & Solos ☐ Improvisation
☐ Other: _____

TECHNIQUE & SKILLS: ☐ Scales ☐ Chords ☐ Arpeggios ☐ Ear Training ☐ Exercises
☐ Rhythm & Reading ☐ Applied Theory ☐ Other: _____

CREATIVITY: ☐ Songwriting ☐ Composition ☐ Improvisation ☐ Listening & Study ☐ Lyrics
☐ Other: _____

PERFORMANCE & PROJECTS: ☐ Recording ☐ Backing Tracks ☐ Group Work ☐ Research
☐ Other: _____

TEACHER / ASSIGNMENTS / IMPROVEMENTS

_____
_____
_____
_____
_____

PROGRESS SNAPSHOT (Circle how today's practice went:)

☹ 🙁 😐 🙂 😄

NEXT PRACTICE GOALS

_____
_____
_____
_____
_____

PRACTICE SESSION

DAY / DATE: _____ INSTRUMENT _____
Motivation: ☐ Low   ☐ Medium   ☐ High

TODAY'S FOCUS

1. _____
2. _____
3. _____

PRACTICE TIME

Planned: ☐ 10   ☐ 20   ☐ 30   ☐ 45   ☐ 60+ minutes   Actual Practice: _____

WHAT YOU PRACTICED TODAY

PLAYING: ☐ New Music ☐ Repertoire ☐ Excerpt Practice ☐ Riffs & Solos ☐ Improvisation
☐ Other: _____

TECHNIQUE & SKILLS: ☐ Scales ☐ Chords ☐ Arpeggios ☐ Ear Training ☐ Exercises
☐ Rhythm & Reading ☐ Applied Theory ☐ Other: _____
_____

CREATIVITY: ☐ Songwriting ☐ Composition ☐ Improvisation ☐ Listening & Study ☐ Lyrics
☐ Other: _____

PERFORMANCE & PROJECTS: ☐ Recording ☐ Backing Tracks ☐ Group Work ☐ Research
☐ Other: _____

TEACHER / ASSIGNMENTS / IMPROVEMENTS

_____
_____
_____
_____
_____

PROGRESS SNAPSHOT (Circle how today's practice went:)

☹   🙁   😐   🙂   😄

NEXT PRACTICE GOALS

_____
_____
_____

DAILY TIP:

The musician must practice until technique is forgotten. Debussy

PRACTICE SUMMARY

DATE RANGE: _____
TOTAL SESSIONS: _____ TOTAL TIME: _____

OVERALL FOCUS / ENERGY THIS PERIOD
☐ Strong Momentum ☐ Balanced Progress ☐ Slower Week ☐ Reset / Recovery

TOP 3 ACCOMPLISHMENTS
1. _____
2. _____
3. _____

WHAT YOU WORKED ON MOST
PLAYING: _____
_____

TECHNIQUE & SKILLS: _____
_____

CREATIVITY: _____
_____

PERFORMANCE & PROJECTS: _____
_____

DEEP PRACTICE RECAP
Piece / Exercise: _____
Current Metronome: _____ bpm   Goal: _____ bpm
Focus Area: ☐ Tone ☐ Timing ☐ Fingering ☐ Articulation ☐ Other
Improvement Plan: _____

PERFORMANCES
☐ Recorded / Video ☐ Played for Someone ☐ Ensemble / Jam ☐ None this Week

PROGRESS & INSIGHTS
What improved the most? _____
What still needs work? _____
Creative discoveries or ideas? _____

NEXT FOCUS / UPCOMING GOALS
_____
_____
_____

WEEKLY INSIGHT
The speed of your progress is less important than the consistency of your effort.

WEEK SUMMARY

PRACTICE SESSION

DAY / DATE: _____ INSTRUMENT _____
Motivation: ☐ Low ☐ Medium ☐ High

TODAY'S FOCUS

1. _____
2. _____
3. _____

PRACTICE TIME

Planned: ☐ 10 ☐ 20 ☐ 30 ☐ 45 ☐ 60+ minutes   Actual Practice: _____

WHAT YOU PRACTICED TODAY

PLAYING: ☐ New Music ☐ Repertoire ☐ Excerpt Practice ☐ Riffs & Solos ☐ Improvisation
☐ Other: _____

TECHNIQUE & SKILLS: ☐ Scales ☐ Chords ☐ Arpeggios ☐ Ear Training ☐ Exercises
☐ Rhythm & Reading ☐ Applied Theory ☐ Other: _____

CREATIVITY: ☐ Songwriting ☐ Composition ☐ Improvisation ☐ Listening & Study ☐ Lyrics
☐ Other: _____

PERFORMANCE & PROJECTS: ☐ Recording ☐ Backing Tracks ☐ Group Work ☐ Research
☐ Other: _____

TEACHER / ASSIGNMENTS / IMPROVEMENTS

_____
_____
_____
_____
_____

PROGRESS SNAPSHOT (Circle how today's practice went:)

☹ 🙁 😐 🙂 😊

NEXT PRACTICE GOALS

_____
_____
_____

DAILY TIP:

Simplicity is the ultimate sophistication. Leonardo da Vinci

PRACTICE SESSION

DAY / DATE: _____ INSTRUMENT _____

Motivation: ☐ Low ☐ Medium ☐ High

TODAY'S FOCUS

1. _____
2. _____
3. _____

PRACTICE TIME

Planned: ☐ 10 ☐ 20 ☐ 30 ☐ 45 ☐ 60+ minutes   Actual Practice: _____

WHAT YOU PRACTICED TODAY

PLAYING: ☐ New Music ☐ Repertoire ☐ Excerpt Practice ☐ Riffs & Solos ☐ Improvisation
☐ Other: _____

TECHNIQUE & SKILLS: ☐ Scales ☐ Chords ☐ Arpeggios ☐ Ear Training ☐ Exercises
☐ Rhythm & Reading ☐ Applied Theory ☐ Other: _____

CREATIVITY: ☐ Songwriting ☐ Composition ☐ Improvisation ☐ Listening & Study ☐ Lyrics
☐ Other: _____

PERFORMANCE & PROJECTS: ☐ Recording ☐ Backing Tracks ☐ Group Work ☐ Research
☐ Other: _____

TEACHER / ASSIGNMENTS / IMPROVEMENTS

_____
_____
_____
_____
_____

PROGRESS SNAPSHOT (Circle how today's practice went:)

☹ 🙁 😐 🙂 😃

NEXT PRACTICE GOALS

_____
_____
_____
_____
_____

DAY SESSION

PRACTICE SESSION

DAY / DATE: _____ INSTRUMENT _____
Motivation: ☐ Low ☐ Medium ☐ High

TODAY'S FOCUS

1. _____
2. _____
3. _____

PRACTICE TIME

Planned: ☐ 10 ☐ 20 ☐ 30 ☐ 45 ☐ 60+ minutes   Actual Practice: _____

WHAT YOU PRACTICED TODAY

PLAYING: ☐ New Music ☐ Repertoire ☐ Excerpt Practice ☐ Riffs & Solos ☐ Improvisation
☐ Other: _____

TECHNIQUE & SKILLS: ☐ Scales ☐ Chords ☐ Arpeggios ☐ Ear Training ☐ Exercises
☐ Rhythm & Reading ☐ Applied Theory ☐ Other: _____
_____

CREATIVITY: ☐ Songwriting ☐ Composition ☐ Improvisation ☐ Listening & Study ☐ Lyrics
☐ Other: _____

PERFORMANCE & PROJECTS: ☐ Recording ☐ Backing Tracks ☐ Group Work ☐ Research
☐ Other: _____

TEACHER / ASSIGNMENTS / IMPROVEMENTS

_____
_____
_____
_____
_____

PROGRESS SNAPSHOT (Circle how today's practice went:)

☹ 🙁 😐 🙂 😊

NEXT PRACTICE GOALS

_____
_____
_____

DAILY TIP:

The hand learns what the ear demands.

PRACTICE SESSION

DAY / DATE: _____ INSTRUMENT _____
Motivation: ☐ Low ☐ Medium ☐ High

TODAY'S FOCUS
1. _____
2. _____
3. _____

PRACTICE TIME
Planned: ☐ 10 ☐ 20 ☐ 30 ☐ 45 ☐ 60+ minutes   Actual Practice: _____

WHAT YOU PRACTICED TODAY

PLAYING: ☐ New Music ☐ Repertoire ☐ Excerpt Practice ☐ Riffs & Solos ☐ Improvisation
☐ Other: _____

TECHNIQUE & SKILLS: ☐ Scales ☐ Chords ☐ Arpeggios ☐ Ear Training ☐ Exercises
☐ Rhythm & Reading ☐ Applied Theory ☐ Other:_____

CREATIVITY: ☐ Songwriting ☐ Composition ☐ Improvisation ☐ Listening & Study ☐ Lyrics
☐ Other: _____

PERFORMANCE & PROJECTS: ☐ Recording ☐ Backing Tracks ☐ Group Work ☐ Research
☐ Other: _____

TEACHER / ASSIGNMENTS / IMPROVEMENTS
_____
_____
_____
_____
_____

PROGRESS SNAPSHOT (Circle how today's practice went:)

😠   😕   😐   🙂   😃

NEXT PRACTICE GOALS
_____
_____
_____
_____
_____

DAY SESSION

PRACTICE SESSION

DAY / DATE: _____ INSTRUMENT _____
Motivation: ☐ Low ☐ Medium ☐ High

TODAY'S FOCUS

1. _____
2. _____
3. _____

PRACTICE TIME

Planned: ☐ 10 ☐ 20 ☐ 30 ☐ 45 ☐ 60+ minutes   Actual Practice: _____

WHAT YOU PRACTICED TODAY

PLAYING: ☐ New Music ☐ Repertoire ☐ Excerpt Practice ☐ Riffs & Solos ☐ Improvisation
☐ Other: _____

TECHNIQUE & SKILLS: ☐ Scales ☐ Chords ☐ Arpeggios ☐ Ear Training ☐ Exercises
☐ Rhythm & Reading ☐ Applied Theory ☐ Other: _____

CREATIVITY: ☐ Songwriting ☐ Composition ☐ Improvisation ☐ Listening & Study ☐ Lyrics
☐ Other: _____

PERFORMANCE & PROJECTS: ☐ Recording ☐ Backing Tracks ☐ Group Work ☐ Research
☐ Other: _____

TEACHER / ASSIGNMENTS / IMPROVEMENTS

_____
_____
_____
_____
_____

PROGRESS SNAPSHOT (Circle how today's practice went:)

☹ ☹ 😐 🙂 😊

NEXT PRACTICE GOALS

_____
_____
_____

DAILY TIP:

Practice arpeggios as melodies, not drills.

PRACTICE SUMMARY

DATE RANGE: _____
TOTAL SESSIONS: _____ TOTAL TIME: _____

OVERALL FOCUS / ENERGY THIS PERIOD
☐ Strong Momentum ☐ Balanced Progress ☐ Slower Week ☐ Reset / Recovery

TOP 3 ACCOMPLISHMENTS
1. _____
2. _____
3. _____

WHAT YOU WORKED ON MOST
PLAYING: _____
_____

TECHNIQUE & SKILLS: _____
_____

CREATIVITY: _____
_____

PERFORMANCE & PROJECTS: _____
_____

DEEP PRACTICE RECAP
Piece / Exercise: _____
Current Metronome: _____ bpm   Goal: _____ bpm
Focus Area: ☐ Tone ☐ Timing ☐ Fingering ☐ Articulation ☐ Other
Improvement Plan: _____

PERFORMANCES
☐ Recorded / Video ☐ Played for Someone ☐ Ensemble / Jam ☐ None this Week

PROGRESS & INSIGHTS
What improved the most? _____
What still needs work? _____
Creative discoveries or ideas? _____

NEXT FOCUS / UPCOMING GOALS
_____
_____
_____

WEEKLY INSIGHT
Write down one moment this week where the music felt effortless.
Can you reverse-engineer the mental state that created that flow?

WEEK SUMMARY

TEACHER / LESSON NOTES

LESSON DATE: _____ INSTRUMENT _____
Readiness:　☐ Low　☐ Medium　☐ High

ASSIGNMENTS / FOCUS POINTS

1. _____
2. _____
3. _____
4. _____
5. _____

HOW LONG YOU SHOULD PRACTICE AT EACH SESSION

Planned:　☐ 10　☐ 20　☐ 30　☐ 45　☐ 60+ minutes　Other: _____

TECHNIQUE & SKILLS: ☐ Scales　☐ Chords　☐ Arpeggios　☐ Ear Training　☐ Exercises
☐ Rhythm & Reading　☐ Applied Theory　☐ Other: _____
_____
_____

REPERTOIRE 1
Title / Section: _____
Measures / Focus: _____ Tempo Goal: _____ bpm

REPERTOIRE 2
Title / Section: _____
Measures / Focus: _____ Tempo Goal: _____ bpm

REPERTOIRE 3
Title / Section: _____
Measures / Focus: _____ Tempo Goal: _____ bpm

TEACHER COMMENTS
_____
_____
_____
_____
_____

STUDENT NOTES
_____
_____
_____

IDEAS & NOTES

PRACTICE SESSION

DAY / DATE: _____   INSTRUMENT _____

Motivation: ☐ Low   ☐ Medium   ☐ High

TODAY'S FOCUS

1. _____
2. _____
3. _____

PRACTICE TIME

Planned: ☐ 10   ☐ 20   ☐ 30   ☐ 45   ☐ 60+ minutes   Actual Practice: _____

WHAT YOU PRACTICED TODAY

PLAYING: ☐ New Music   ☐ Repertoire   ☐ Excerpt Practice   ☐ Riffs & Solos   ☐ Improvisation
☐ Other: _____

TECHNIQUE & SKILLS: ☐ Scales   ☐ Chords   ☐ Arpeggios   ☐ Ear Training   ☐ Exercises
☐ Rhythm & Reading   ☐ Applied Theory   ☐ Other: _____

CREATIVITY: ☐ Songwriting   ☐ Composition   ☐ Improvisation   ☐ Listening & Study   ☐ Lyrics
☐ Other: _____

PERFORMANCE & PROJECTS: ☐ Recording   ☐ Backing Tracks   ☐ Group Work   ☐ Research
☐ Other: _____

TEACHER / ASSIGNMENTS / IMPROVEMENTS

_____
_____
_____
_____
_____

PROGRESS SNAPSHOT (Circle how today's practice went:)

☹   🙁   😐   🙂   😄

NEXT PRACTICE GOALS

_____
_____
_____

DAILY TIP:

The journey of a thousand songs begins with the first note.

PRACTICE SESSION

DAY / DATE: _____ INSTRUMENT _____

Motivation: ☐ Low   ☐ Medium   ☐ High

TODAY'S FOCUS
1. _____
2. _____
3. _____

PRACTICE TIME
Planned: ☐ 10 ☐ 20 ☐ 30 ☐ 45 ☐ 60+ minutes   Actual Practice: _____

WHAT YOU PRACTICED TODAY

PLAYING: ☐ New Music ☐ Repertoire ☐ Excerpt Practice ☐ Riffs & Solos ☐ Improvisation
☐ Other: _____

TECHNIQUE & SKILLS: ☐ Scales ☐ Chords ☐ Arpeggios ☐ Ear Training ☐ Exercises
☐ Rhythm & Reading ☐ Applied Theory ☐ Other: _____

CREATIVITY: ☐ Songwriting ☐ Composition ☐ Improvisation ☐ Listening & Study ☐ Lyrics
☐ Other: _____

PERFORMANCE & PROJECTS: ☐ Recording ☐ Backing Tracks ☐ Group Work ☐ Research
☐ Other: _____

TEACHER / ASSIGNMENTS / IMPROVEMENTS
_____
_____
_____
_____
_____

PROGRESS SNAPSHOT (Circle how today's practice went:)

☹   🙁   😐   🙂   😄

NEXT PRACTICE GOALS
_____
_____
_____
_____
_____

DAY SESSION

PRACTICE SESSION

DAY / DATE: _____ INSTRUMENT _____
Motivation: ☐ Low ☐ Medium ☐ High

TODAY'S FOCUS

1. _____
2. _____
3. _____

PRACTICE TIME

Planned: ☐ 10 ☐ 20 ☐ 30 ☐ 45 ☐ 60+ minutes   Actual Practice: _____

WHAT YOU PRACTICED TODAY

PLAYING: ☐ New Music ☐ Repertoire ☐ Excerpt Practice ☐ Riffs & Solos ☐ Improvisation
☐ Other: _____

TECHNIQUE & SKILLS: ☐ Scales ☐ Chords ☐ Arpeggios ☐ Ear Training ☐ Exercises
☐ Rhythm & Reading ☐ Applied Theory ☐ Other: _____
_____

CREATIVITY: ☐ Songwriting ☐ Composition ☐ Improvisation ☐ Listening & Study ☐ Lyrics
☐ Other: _____

PERFORMANCE & PROJECTS: ☐ Recording ☐ Backing Tracks ☐ Group Work ☐ Research
☐ Other: _____

TEACHER / ASSIGNMENTS / IMPROVEMENTS

_____
_____
_____
_____
_____

PROGRESS SNAPSHOT (Circle how today's practice went:)

☹ 🙁 😐 🙂 😃

NEXT PRACTICE GOALS

_____
_____
_____

DAILY TIP:

Reverse-engineer your favourite song: ask yourself what makes it great.

PRACTICE SESSION

DAY / DATE: _____ INSTRUMENT _____
Motivation: ☐ Low ☐ Medium ☐ High

TODAY'S FOCUS
1. _____
2. _____
3. _____

PRACTICE TIME
Planned: ☐ 10 ☐ 20 ☐ 30 ☐ 45 ☐ 60+ minutes   Actual Practice: _____

WHAT YOU PRACTICED TODAY

PLAYING: ☐ New Music ☐ Repertoire ☐ Excerpt Practice ☐ Riffs & Solos ☐ Improvisation
☐ Other: _____

TECHNIQUE & SKILLS: ☐ Scales ☐ Chords ☐ Arpeggios ☐ Ear Training ☐ Exercises
☐ Rhythm & Reading ☐ Applied Theory ☐ Other: _____

CREATIVITY: ☐ Songwriting ☐ Composition ☐ Improvisation ☐ Listening & Study ☐ Lyrics
☐ Other: _____

PERFORMANCE & PROJECTS: ☐ Recording ☐ Backing Tracks ☐ Group Work ☐ Research
☐ Other: _____

TEACHER / ASSIGNMENTS / IMPROVEMENTS
_____
_____
_____
_____
_____

PROGRESS SNAPSHOT (Circle how today's practice went:)

☹   🙁   😐   🙂   😀

NEXT PRACTICE GOALS
_____
_____
_____
_____
_____

DAY SESSION

PRACTICE SESSION

DAY / DATE: _____ INSTRUMENT _____
Motivation: ☐ Low ☐ Medium ☐ High

TODAY'S FOCUS
1. _____
2. _____
3. _____

PRACTICE TIME
Planned: ☐ 10 ☐ 20 ☐ 30 ☐ 45 ☐ 60+ minutes   Actual Practice: _____

WHAT YOU PRACTICED TODAY

PLAYING: ☐ New Music ☐ Repertoire ☐ Excerpt Practice ☐ Riffs & Solos ☐ Improvisation
☐ Other: _____

TECHNIQUE & SKILLS: ☐ Scales ☐ Chords ☐ Arpeggios ☐ Ear Training ☐ Exercises
☐ Rhythm & Reading ☐ Applied Theory ☐ Other: _____

CREATIVITY: ☐ Songwriting ☐ Composition ☐ Improvisation ☐ Listening & Study ☐ Lyrics
☐ Other: _____

PERFORMANCE & PROJECTS: ☐ Recording ☐ Backing Tracks ☐ Group Work ☐ Research
☐ Other: _____

TEACHER / ASSIGNMENTS / IMPROVEMENTS
_____
_____
_____
_____
_____

PROGRESS SNAPSHOT (Circle how today's practice went:)

☹ 🙁 😐 🙂 😊

NEXT PRACTICE GOALS
_____
_____
_____

DAILY TIP:

Expression blossoms from discipline. Liszt

PRACTICE SUMMARY

DATE RANGE: _____
TOTAL SESSIONS: _____ TOTAL TIME: _____

OVERALL FOCUS / ENERGY THIS PERIOD
☐ Strong Momentum ☐ Balanced Progress ☐ Slower Week ☐ Reset / Recovery

TOP 3 ACCOMPLISHMENTS
1. _____
2. _____
3. _____

WHAT YOU WORKED ON MOST

PLAYING: _____
_____

TECHNIQUE & SKILLS: _____
_____

CREATIVITY: _____
_____

PERFORMANCE & PROJECTS: _____
_____

DEEP PRACTICE RECAP
Piece / Exercise: _____
Current Metronome: _____ bpm   Goal: _____ bpm
Focus Area: ☐ Tone ☐ Timing ☐ Fingering ☐ Articulation ☐ Other
Improvement Plan: _____

PERFORMANCES
☐ Recorded / Video ☐ Played for Someone ☐ Ensemble / Jam ☐ None this Week

PROGRESS & INSIGHTS
What improved the most? _____
What still needs work? _____
Creative discoveries or ideas? _____

NEXT FOCUS / UPCOMING GOALS
_____
_____
_____

WEEKLY INSIGHT
Look back at your log. If you were your own teacher, what single piece of advice would you give yourself for the upcoming week?

PRACTICE SESSION

DAY / DATE: _____ INSTRUMENT _____
Motivation: ☐ Low ☐ Medium ☐ High

TODAY'S FOCUS

1. _____
2. _____
3. _____

PRACTICE TIME

Planned: ☐ 10 ☐ 20 ☐ 30 ☐ 45 ☐ 60+ minutes   Actual Practice: _____

WHAT YOU PRACTICED TODAY

PLAYING: ☐ New Music ☐ Repertoire ☐ Excerpt Practice ☐ Riffs & Solos ☐ Improvisation
☐ Other: _____

TECHNIQUE & SKILLS: ☐ Scales ☐ Chords ☐ Arpeggios ☐ Ear Training ☐ Exercises
☐ Rhythm & Reading ☐ Applied Theory ☐ Other: _____

CREATIVITY: ☐ Songwriting ☐ Composition ☐ Improvisation ☐ Listening & Study ☐ Lyrics
☐ Other: _____

PERFORMANCE & PROJECTS: ☐ Recording ☐ Backing Tracks ☐ Group Work ☐ Research
☐ Other: _____

TEACHER / ASSIGNMENTS / IMPROVEMENTS

_____
_____
_____
_____
_____

PROGRESS SNAPSHOT (Circle how today's practice went:)

😠 ☹ 😐 🙂 😄

NEXT PRACTICE GOALS

_____
_____
_____

DAILY TIP:

Words are not music.

PRACTICE SESSION

DAY / DATE: _____ INSTRUMENT _____
Motivation: ☐ Low ☐ Medium ☐ High

TODAY'S FOCUS
1. _____
2. _____
3. _____

PRACTICE TIME
Planned: ☐ 10 ☐ 20 ☐ 30 ☐ 45 ☐ 60+ minutes   Actual Practice: _____

WHAT YOU PRACTICED TODAY

PLAYING: ☐ New Music ☐ Repertoire ☐ Excerpt Practice ☐ Riffs & Solos ☐ Improvisation
☐ Other: _____

TECHNIQUE & SKILLS: ☐ Scales ☐ Chords ☐ Arpeggios ☐ Ear Training ☐ Exercises
☐ Rhythm & Reading ☐ Applied Theory ☐ Other: _____

CREATIVITY: ☐ Songwriting ☐ Composition ☐ Improvisation ☐ Listening & Study ☐ Lyrics
☐ Other: _____

PERFORMANCE & PROJECTS: ☐ Recording ☐ Backing Tracks ☐ Group Work ☐ Research
☐ Other: _____

TEACHER / ASSIGNMENTS / IMPROVEMENTS
_____
_____
_____
_____
_____

PROGRESS SNAPSHOT (Circle how today's practice went:)

☹ 🙁 😐 🙂 😊

NEXT PRACTICE GOALS
_____
_____
_____
_____
_____

DAY SESSION

PRACTICE SESSION

DAY / DATE: _____ INSTRUMENT _____

Motivation: ☐ Low ☐ Medium ☐ High

TODAY'S FOCUS

1. _____
2. _____
3. _____

PRACTICE TIME

Planned: ☐ 10 ☐ 20 ☐ 30 ☐ 45 ☐ 60+ minutes   Actual Practice: _____

WHAT YOU PRACTICED TODAY

PLAYING: ☐ New Music ☐ Repertoire ☐ Excerpt Practice ☐ Riffs & Solos ☐ Improvisation
☐ Other: _____

TECHNIQUE & SKILLS: ☐ Scales ☐ Chords ☐ Arpeggios ☐ Ear Training ☐ Exercises
☐ Rhythm & Reading ☐ Applied Theory ☐ Other: _____
_____

CREATIVITY: ☐ Songwriting ☐ Composition ☐ Improvisation ☐ Listening & Study ☐ Lyrics
☐ Other: _____

PERFORMANCE & PROJECTS: ☐ Recording ☐ Backing Tracks ☐ Group Work ☐ Research
☐ Other: _____

TEACHER / ASSIGNMENTS / IMPROVEMENTS

_____
_____
_____
_____
_____

PROGRESS SNAPSHOT (Circle how today's practice went:)

☹ 🙁 😐 🙂 😊

NEXT PRACTICE GOALS

_____
_____
_____

DAILY TIP:

Music begins where words end. Heinrich Heine

PRACTICE SESSION

DAY / DATE: _____ INSTRUMENT _____
Motivation: ☐ Low   ☐ Medium   ☐ High

TODAY'S FOCUS
1. _____
2. _____
3. _____

PRACTICE TIME
Planned: ☐ 10 ☐ 20 ☐ 30 ☐ 45 ☐ 60+ minutes   Actual Practice: _____

WHAT YOU PRACTICED TODAY

PLAYING: ☐ New Music ☐ Repertoire ☐ Excerpt Practice ☐ Riffs & Solos ☐ Improvisation
☐ Other: _____

TECHNIQUE & SKILLS: ☐ Scales ☐ Chords ☐ Arpeggios ☐ Ear Training ☐ Exercises
☐ Rhythm & Reading ☐ Applied Theory ☐ Other: _____

CREATIVITY: ☐ Songwriting ☐ Composition ☐ Improvisation ☐ Listening & Study ☐ Lyrics
☐ Other: _____

PERFORMANCE & PROJECTS: ☐ Recording ☐ Backing Tracks ☐ Group Work ☐ Research
☐ Other: _____

TEACHER / ASSIGNMENTS / IMPROVEMENTS
_____
_____
_____
_____
_____

PROGRESS SNAPSHOT (Circle how today's practice went:)

☹   🙁   😐   🙂   😃

NEXT PRACTICE GOALS
_____
_____
_____
_____
_____

DAY SESSION

PRACTICE SESSION

DAY / DATE: _____ INSTRUMENT _____

Motivation: ☐ Low   ☐ Medium   ☐ High

TODAY'S FOCUS

1. _____
2. _____
3. _____

PRACTICE TIME

Planned: ☐ 10 ☐ 20 ☐ 30 ☐ 45 ☐ 60+ minutes   Actual Practice: _____

WHAT YOU PRACTICED TODAY

PLAYING: ☐ New Music ☐ Repertoire ☐ Excerpt Practice ☐ Riffs & Solos ☐ Improvisation
☐ Other: _____

TECHNIQUE & SKILLS: ☐ Scales ☐ Chords ☐ Arpeggios ☐ Ear Training ☐ Exercises
☐ Rhythm & Reading ☐ Applied Theory ☐ Other: _____

CREATIVITY: ☐ Songwriting ☐ Composition ☐ Improvisation ☐ Listening & Study ☐ Lyrics
☐ Other: _____

PERFORMANCE & PROJECTS: ☐ Recording ☐ Backing Tracks ☐ Group Work ☐ Research
☐ Other: _____

TEACHER / ASSIGNMENTS / IMPROVEMENTS

_____
_____
_____
_____
_____

PROGRESS SNAPSHOT (Circle how today's practice went:)

☹   🙁   😐   🙂   😊

NEXT PRACTICE GOALS

_____
_____
_____

DAILY TIP:

Great things are done by a series of small things. Vincent van Gogh

PRACTICE SUMMARY

DATE RANGE: _____
TOTAL SESSIONS: _____ TOTAL TIME: _____

OVERALL FOCUS / ENERGY THIS PERIOD
☐ Strong Momentum ☐ Balanced Progress ☐ Slower Week ☐ Reset / Recovery

TOP 3 ACCOMPLISHMENTS
1. _____
2. _____
3. _____

WHAT YOU WORKED ON MOST
PLAYING: _____
_____

TECHNIQUE & SKILLS: _____
_____

CREATIVITY: _____
_____

PERFORMANCE & PROJECTS: _____
_____

DEEP PRACTICE RECAP
Piece / Exercise: _____
Current Metronome: _____ bpm   Goal: _____ bpm
Focus Area: ☐ Tone ☐ Timing ☐ Fingering ☐ Articulation ☐ Other
Improvement Plan: _____

PERFORMANCES
☐ Recorded / Video ☐ Played for Someone ☐ Ensemble / Jam ☐ None this Week

PROGRESS & INSIGHTS
What improved the most? _____
What still needs work? _____
Creative discoveries or ideas? _____

NEXT FOCUS / UPCOMING GOALS
_____
_____
_____

WEEKLY INSIGHT
Identify the perfect excuse you used to skip practicing for a full session.

WEEK SUMMARY

TEACHER / LESSON NOTES

LESSON DATE: _____ INSTRUMENT _____
Readiness: ☐ Low ☐ Medium ☐ High

ASSIGNMENTS / FOCUS POINTS
1. _____
2. _____
3. _____
4. _____
5. _____

HOW LONG YOU SHOULD PRACTICE AT EACH SESSION
Planned: ☐ 10 ☐ 20 ☐ 30 ☐ 45 ☐ 60+ minutes Other: _____

TECHNIQUE & SKILLS: ☐ Scales ☐ Chords ☐ Arpeggios ☐ Ear Training ☐ Exercises
☐ Rhythm & Reading ☐ Applied Theory ☐ Other: _____
_____
_____

REPERTOIRE 1
Title / Section: _____
Measures / Focus: _____ Tempo Goal: _____ bpm

REPERTOIRE 2
Title / Section: _____
Measures / Focus: _____ Tempo Goal: _____ bpm

REPERTOIRE 3
Title / Section: _____
Measures / Focus: _____ Tempo Goal: _____ bpm

TEACHER COMMENTS
_____
_____
_____
_____
_____

STUDENT NOTES
_____
_____
_____

IDEAS & NOTES

MONTHLY REFLECTION

MONTH: _____ TOTAL TIME: _____
TOTAL SESSIONS: _____ TOTAL PERFORMANCES: _____

RATE YOUR PROGRESS THIS MONTH: BELOW ★   AVERAGE ★ ★   ABOVE ★ ★ ★

WHAT ARE YOU MOST GRATEFUL FOR WITH YOUR MUSIC THIS MONTH

_____
_____
_____
_____
_____

SET YOUR GOALS FOR NEXT MONTH

_____
_____
_____
_____
_____

POSITIVE LESSONS OR HABITS TO CONTINUE NEXT MONTH

_____
_____
_____
_____
_____

NOTES

_____
_____
_____
_____

INSIGHT

Stop thinking of practice as something you have to do. Start thinking of it as who you are as a musician.

*When everything feels tangled,
connect two ideas that belong together.
That connection is enough to restart.*

PRACTICE SESSION

DAY / DATE: _____ INSTRUMENT _____
Motivation: ☐ Low ☐ Medium ☐ High

TODAY'S FOCUS
1. _____
2. _____
3. _____

PRACTICE TIME
Planned: ☐ 10 ☐ 20 ☐ 30 ☐ 45 ☐ 60+ minutes   Actual Practice: _____

WHAT YOU PRACTICED TODAY

PLAYING: ☐ New Music ☐ Repertoire ☐ Excerpt Practice ☐ Riffs & Solos ☐ Improvisation
☐ Other: _____

TECHNIQUE & SKILLS: ☐ Scales ☐ Chords ☐ Arpeggios ☐ Ear Training ☐ Exercises
☐ Rhythm & Reading ☐ Applied Theory ☐ Other: _____
_____

CREATIVITY: ☐ Songwriting ☐ Composition ☐ Improvisation ☐ Listening & Study ☐ Lyrics
☐ Other: _____

PERFORMANCE & PROJECTS: ☐ Recording ☐ Backing Tracks ☐ Group Work ☐ Research
☐ Other: _____

TEACHER / ASSIGNMENTS / IMPROVEMENTS
_____
_____
_____
_____
_____

PROGRESS SNAPSHOT (Circle how today's practice went:)

☹ 🙁 😐 🙂 😊

NEXT PRACTICE GOALS
_____
_____
_____

DAILY TIP:
Reflect on a note mistake. Don't just fix it; understand the root cause.

PRACTICE SESSION

DAY / DATE: _____ INSTRUMENT _____

Motivation: ☐ Low ☐ Medium ☐ High

TODAY'S FOCUS

1. _____
2. _____
3. _____

PRACTICE TIME

Planned: ☐ 10 ☐ 20 ☐ 30 ☐ 45 ☐ 60+ minutes   Actual Practice: _____

WHAT YOU PRACTICED TODAY

PLAYING: ☐ New Music ☐ Repertoire ☐ Excerpt Practice ☐ Riffs & Solos ☐ Improvisation
☐ Other: _____

TECHNIQUE & SKILLS: ☐ Scales ☐ Chords ☐ Arpeggios ☐ Ear Training ☐ Exercises
☐ Rhythm & Reading ☐ Applied Theory ☐ Other: _____

CREATIVITY: ☐ Songwriting ☐ Composition ☐ Improvisation ☐ Listening & Study ☐ Lyrics
☐ Other: _____

PERFORMANCE & PROJECTS: ☐ Recording ☐ Backing Tracks ☐ Group Work ☐ Research
☐ Other: _____

TEACHER / ASSIGNMENTS / IMPROVEMENTS

_____
_____
_____
_____
_____

PROGRESS SNAPSHOT (Circle how today's practice went:)

😠   🙁   😐   🙂   😄

NEXT PRACTICE GOALS

_____
_____
_____
_____
_____

DAY SESSION

PRACTICE SESSION

DAY / DATE: _____ INSTRUMENT _____
Motivation: ☐ Low ☐ Medium ☐ High

TODAY'S FOCUS

1. _____
2. _____
3. _____

PRACTICE TIME

Planned: ☐ 10 ☐ 20 ☐ 30 ☐ 45 ☐ 60+ minutes   Actual Practice: _____

WHAT YOU PRACTICED TODAY

PLAYING: ☐ New Music ☐ Repertoire ☐ Excerpt Practice ☐ Riffs & Solos ☐ Improvisation
☐ Other: _____

TECHNIQUE & SKILLS: ☐ Scales ☐ Chords ☐ Arpeggios ☐ Ear Training ☐ Exercises
☐ Rhythm & Reading ☐ Applied Theory ☐ Other: _____
_____

CREATIVITY: ☐ Songwriting ☐ Composition ☐ Improvisation ☐ Listening & Study ☐ Lyrics
☐ Other: _____

PERFORMANCE & PROJECTS: ☐ Recording ☐ Backing Tracks ☐ Group Work ☐ Research
☐ Other: _____

TEACHER / ASSIGNMENTS / IMPROVEMENTS

_____
_____
_____
_____
_____

PROGRESS SNAPSHOT (Circle how today's practice went:)

😠 ☹️ 😐 🙂 😄

NEXT PRACTICE GOALS

_____
_____
_____

DAILY TIP:
One measure perfected beats a page half-learned.

PRACTICE SESSION

DAY / DATE: _____ INSTRUMENT _____
Motivation: ☐ Low ☐ Medium ☐ High

TODAY'S FOCUS
1. _____
2. _____
3. _____

PRACTICE TIME
Planned: ☐ 10 ☐ 20 ☐ 30 ☐ 45 ☐ 60+ minutes   Actual Practice: _____

WHAT YOU PRACTICED TODAY

PLAYING: ☐ New Music ☐ Repertoire ☐ Excerpt Practice ☐ Riffs & Solos ☐ Improvisation
☐ Other: _____

TECHNIQUE & SKILLS: ☐ Scales ☐ Chords ☐ Arpeggios ☐ Ear Training ☐ Exercises
☐ Rhythm & Reading ☐ Applied Theory ☐ Other: _____

CREATIVITY: ☐ Songwriting ☐ Composition ☐ Improvisation ☐ Listening & Study ☐ Lyrics
☐ Other: _____

PERFORMANCE & PROJECTS: ☐ Recording ☐ Backing Tracks ☐ Group Work ☐ Research
☐ Other: _____

TEACHER / ASSIGNMENTS / IMPROVEMENTS
_____
_____
_____
_____

PROGRESS SNAPSHOT (Circle how today's practice went:)

😠   ☹️   😐   🙂   😄

NEXT PRACTICE GOALS
_____
_____
_____
_____

DAY SESSION

PRACTICE SESSION

DAY / DATE: _____ INSTRUMENT _____
Motivation: ☐ Low ☐ Medium ☐ High

TODAY'S FOCUS

1. _____
2. _____
3. _____

PRACTICE TIME

Planned: ☐ 10 ☐ 20 ☐ 30 ☐ 45 ☐ 60+ minutes   Actual Practice: _____

WHAT YOU PRACTICED TODAY

PLAYING: ☐ New Music ☐ Repertoire ☐ Excerpt Practice ☐ Riffs & Solos ☐ Improvisation
☐ Other: _____

TECHNIQUE & SKILLS: ☐ Scales ☐ Chords ☐ Arpeggios ☐ Ear Training ☐ Exercises
☐ Rhythm & Reading ☐ Applied Theory ☐ Other: _____
_____

CREATIVITY: ☐ Songwriting ☐ Composition ☐ Improvisation ☐ Listening & Study ☐ Lyrics
☐ Other: _____

PERFORMANCE & PROJECTS: ☐ Recording ☐ Backing Tracks ☐ Group Work ☐ Research
☐ Other: _____

TEACHER / ASSIGNMENTS / IMPROVEMENTS

_____
_____
_____
_____
_____

PROGRESS SNAPSHOT (Circle how today's practice went:)

☹ 🙁 😐 🙂 😃

NEXT PRACTICE GOALS

_____
_____
_____

DAILY TIP:

The audience feels your energy before you play a single note.

PRACTICE SUMMARY

DATE RANGE: _____
TOTAL SESSIONS: _____ TOTAL TIME: _____

OVERALL FOCUS / ENERGY THIS PERIOD
☐ Strong Momentum ☐ Balanced Progress ☐ Slower Week ☐ Reset / Recovery

TOP 3 ACCOMPLISHMENTS
1. _____
2. _____
3. _____

WHAT YOU WORKED ON MOST

PLAYING: _____
_____

TECHNIQUE & SKILLS: _____
_____

CREATIVITY: _____
_____

PERFORMANCE & PROJECTS: _____
_____

DEEP PRACTICE RECAP
Piece / Exercise: _____
Current Metronome: _____ bpm   Goal: _____ bpm
Focus Area: ☐ Tone ☐ Timing ☐ Fingering ☐ Articulation ☐ Other
Improvement Plan: _____

PERFORMANCES
☐ Recorded / Video ☐ Played for Someone ☐ Ensemble / Jam ☐ None this Week

PROGRESS & INSIGHTS
What improved the most? _____
What still needs work? _____
Creative discoveries or ideas? _____

NEXT FOCUS / UPCOMING GOALS
_____
_____
_____

WEEKLY INSIGHT
If you had to fail next week, what single step would you take today to guarantee it?

PRACTICE SESSION

DAY / DATE: _____ INSTRUMENT _____
Motivation: ☐ Low   ☐ Medium   ☐ High

TODAY'S FOCUS

1. _____
2. _____
3. _____

PRACTICE TIME

Planned: ☐ 10   ☐ 20   ☐ 30   ☐ 45   ☐ 60+ minutes   Actual Practice: _____

WHAT YOU PRACTICED TODAY

PLAYING: ☐ New Music   ☐ Repertoire   ☐ Excerpt Practice   ☐ Riffs & Solos   ☐ Improvisation
☐ Other: _____

TECHNIQUE & SKILLS: ☐ Scales   ☐ Chords   ☐ Arpeggios   ☐ Ear Training   ☐ Exercises
☐ Rhythm & Reading   ☐ Applied Theory   ☐ Other: _____

CREATIVITY: ☐ Songwriting   ☐ Composition   ☐ Improvisation   ☐ Listening & Study   ☐ Lyrics
☐ Other: _____

PERFORMANCE & PROJECTS: ☐ Recording   ☐ Backing Tracks   ☐ Group Work   ☐ Research
☐ Other: _____

TEACHER / ASSIGNMENTS / IMPROVEMENTS

_____
_____
_____
_____
_____

PROGRESS SNAPSHOT (Circle how today's practice went:)

☹   🙁   😐   🙂   😊

NEXT PRACTICE GOALS

_____
_____
_____

DAILY TIP:

Every time you stop to fix a mistake, you're practicing stopping. Practice flowing through the music instead.

PRACTICE SESSION

DAY / DATE: _____ INSTRUMENT _____
Motivation: ☐ Low   ☐ Medium   ☐ High

TODAY'S FOCUS
1. _____
2. _____
3. _____

PRACTICE TIME
Planned: ☐ 10 ☐ 20 ☐ 30 ☐ 45 ☐ 60+ minutes   Actual Practice: _____

WHAT YOU PRACTICED TODAY

PLAYING: ☐ New Music ☐ Repertoire ☐ Excerpt Practice ☐ Riffs & Solos ☐ Improvisation
☐ Other: _____

TECHNIQUE & SKILLS: ☐ Scales ☐ Chords ☐ Arpeggios ☐ Ear Training ☐ Exercises
☐ Rhythm & Reading ☐ Applied Theory ☐ Other: _____

CREATIVITY: ☐ Songwriting ☐ Composition ☐ Improvisation ☐ Listening & Study ☐ Lyrics
☐ Other: _____

PERFORMANCE & PROJECTS: ☐ Recording ☐ Backing Tracks ☐ Group Work ☐ Research
☐ Other: _____

TEACHER / ASSIGNMENTS / IMPROVEMENTS
_____
_____
_____
_____
_____

PROGRESS SNAPSHOT (Circle how today's practice went:)

😠   ☹   😐   🙂   😄

NEXT PRACTICE GOALS
_____
_____
_____
_____
_____

PRACTICE SESSION

DAY / DATE: _____ INSTRUMENT _____
Motivation: ☐ Low ☐ Medium ☐ High

TODAY'S FOCUS
1. _____
2. _____
3. _____

PRACTICE TIME
Planned: ☐ 10 ☐ 20 ☐ 30 ☐ 45 ☐ 60+ minutes   Actual Practice: _____

WHAT YOU PRACTICED TODAY

PLAYING: ☐ New Music ☐ Repertoire ☐ Excerpt Practice ☐ Riffs & Solos ☐ Improvisation
☐ Other: _____

TECHNIQUE & SKILLS: ☐ Scales ☐ Chords ☐ Arpeggios ☐ Ear Training ☐ Exercises
☐ Rhythm & Reading ☐ Applied Theory ☐ Other: _____

CREATIVITY: ☐ Songwriting ☐ Composition ☐ Improvisation ☐ Listening & Study ☐ Lyrics
☐ Other: _____

PERFORMANCE & PROJECTS: ☐ Recording ☐ Backing Tracks ☐ Group Work ☐ Research
☐ Other: _____

TEACHER / ASSIGNMENTS / IMPROVEMENTS
_____
_____
_____
_____
_____

PROGRESS SNAPSHOT (Circle how today's practice went:)

☹   🙁   😐   🙂   😀

NEXT PRACTICE GOALS
_____
_____
_____

DAILY TIP:
Practice what you can't do, not what you can.

PRACTICE SESSION

DAY / DATE: _____ INSTRUMENT _____
Motivation: ☐ Low ☐ Medium ☐ High

TODAY'S FOCUS
1. _____
2. _____
3. _____

PRACTICE TIME
Planned: ☐ 10 ☐ 20 ☐ 30 ☐ 45 ☐ 60+ minutes   Actual Practice: _____

WHAT YOU PRACTICED TODAY

PLAYING: ☐ New Music ☐ Repertoire ☐ Excerpt Practice ☐ Riffs & Solos ☐ Improvisation
☐ Other: _____

TECHNIQUE & SKILLS: ☐ Scales ☐ Chords ☐ Arpeggios ☐ Ear Training ☐ Exercises
☐ Rhythm & Reading ☐ Applied Theory ☐ Other: _____

CREATIVITY: ☐ Songwriting ☐ Composition ☐ Improvisation ☐ Listening & Study ☐ Lyrics
☐ Other: _____

PERFORMANCE & PROJECTS: ☐ Recording ☐ Backing Tracks ☐ Group Work ☐ Research
☐ Other: _____

TEACHER / ASSIGNMENTS / IMPROVEMENTS
_____
_____
_____
_____

PROGRESS SNAPSHOT (Circle how today's practice went:)

☹ ☹ 😐 🙂 😄

NEXT PRACTICE GOALS
_____
_____
_____
_____
_____

DAY SESSION

PRACTICE SESSION

DAY / DATE: _____   INSTRUMENT _____
Motivation: ☐ Low   ☐ Medium   ☐ High

TODAY'S FOCUS

1. _____
2. _____
3. _____

PRACTICE TIME

Planned: ☐ 10   ☐ 20   ☐ 30   ☐ 45   ☐ 60+ minutes   Actual Practice: _____

WHAT YOU PRACTICED TODAY

PLAYING: ☐ New Music   ☐ Repertoire   ☐ Excerpt Practice   ☐ Riffs & Solos   ☐ Improvisation
☐ Other: _____

TECHNIQUE & SKILLS: ☐ Scales   ☐ Chords   ☐ Arpeggios   ☐ Ear Training   ☐ Exercises
☐ Rhythm & Reading   ☐ Applied Theory   ☐ Other: _____
_____

CREATIVITY: ☐ Songwriting   ☐ Composition   ☐ Improvisation   ☐ Listening & Study   ☐ Lyrics
☐ Other: _____

PERFORMANCE & PROJECTS: ☐ Recording   ☐ Backing Tracks   ☐ Group Work   ☐ Research
☐ Other: _____

TEACHER / ASSIGNMENTS / IMPROVEMENTS

_____
_____
_____
_____
_____

PROGRESS SNAPSHOT (Circle how today's practice went:)

☹   🙁   😐   🙂   😄

NEXT PRACTICE GOALS

_____
_____
_____

DAILY TIP:

One who feels it knows it.

PRACTICE SUMMARY

DATE RANGE: _____
TOTAL SESSIONS: _____ TOTAL TIME: _____

OVERALL FOCUS / ENERGY THIS PERIOD
☐ Strong Momentum ☐ Balanced Progress ☐ Slower Week ☐ Reset / Recovery

TOP 3 ACCOMPLISHMENTS
1. _____
2. _____
3. _____

WHAT YOU WORKED ON MOST
PLAYING: _____
_____

TECHNIQUE & SKILLS: _____
_____

CREATIVITY: _____
_____

PERFORMANCE & PROJECTS: _____
_____

DEEP PRACTICE RECAP
Piece / Exercise: _____
Current Metronome: _____ bpm   Goal: _____ bpm
Focus Area: ☐ Tone ☐ Timing ☐ Fingering ☐ Articulation ☐ Other
Improvement Plan: _____

PERFORMANCES
☐ Recorded / Video ☐ Played for Someone ☐ Ensemble / Jam ☐ None this Week

PROGRESS & INSIGHTS
What improved the most? _____
What still needs work? _____
Creative discoveries or ideas? _____

NEXT FOCUS / UPCOMING GOALS
_____
_____
_____

WEEKLY INSIGHT
He who wishes to sing always finds a song. Swedish proverb

TEACHER / LESSON NOTES

LESSON DATE: _____ INSTRUMENT _____
Readiness: ☐ Low   ☐ Medium   ☐ High

ASSIGNMENTS / FOCUS POINTS
1. _____
2. _____
3. _____
4. _____
5. _____

HOW LONG YOU SHOULD PRACTICE AT EACH SESSION
Planned: ☐ 10   ☐ 20   ☐ 30   ☐ 45   ☐ 60+ minutes   Other: _____

TECHNIQUE & SKILLS: ☐ Scales   ☐ Chords   ☐ Arpeggios   ☐ Ear Training   ☐ Exercises
☐ Rhythm & Reading   ☐ Applied Theory   ☐ Other: _____
_____
_____

REPERTOIRE 1
Title / Section: _____
Measures / Focus: _____ Tempo Goal: _____ bpm

REPERTOIRE 2
Title / Section: _____
Measures / Focus: _____ Tempo Goal: _____ bpm

REPERTOIRE 3
Title / Section: _____
Measures / Focus: _____ Tempo Goal: _____ bpm

TEACHER COMMENTS
_____
_____
_____
_____
_____

STUDENT NOTES
_____
_____
_____

IDEAS & NOTES

PRACTICE SESSION

DAY / DATE: _____   INSTRUMENT _____
Motivation: ☐ Low   ☐ Medium   ☐ High

TODAY'S FOCUS

1. _____
2. _____
3. _____

PRACTICE TIME

Planned: ☐ 10   ☐ 20   ☐ 30   ☐ 45   ☐ 60+ minutes   Actual Practice: _____

WHAT YOU PRACTICED TODAY

PLAYING: ☐ New Music ☐ Repertoire ☐ Excerpt Practice ☐ Riffs & Solos ☐ Improvisation
☐ Other: _____

TECHNIQUE & SKILLS: ☐ Scales ☐ Chords ☐ Arpeggios ☐ Ear Training ☐ Exercises
☐ Rhythm & Reading ☐ Applied Theory ☐ Other: _____
_____

CREATIVITY: ☐ Songwriting ☐ Composition ☐ Improvisation ☐ Listening & Study ☐ Lyrics
☐ Other: _____

PERFORMANCE & PROJECTS: ☐ Recording ☐ Backing Tracks ☐ Group Work ☐ Research
☐ Other: _____

TEACHER / ASSIGNMENTS / IMPROVEMENTS

_____
_____
_____
_____
_____
_____

PROGRESS SNAPSHOT (Circle how today's practice went:)

☹   🙁   😐   🙂   😊

NEXT PRACTICE GOALS

_____
_____
_____

DAILY TIP:

Work on easy pieces until mastered, medium pieces until they become easy, and difficult pieces until they become medium.

PRACTICE SESSION

DAY / DATE: _____ INSTRUMENT _____

Motivation: ☐ Low ☐ Medium ☐ High

TODAY'S FOCUS

1. _____
2. _____
3. _____

PRACTICE TIME

Planned: ☐ 10 ☐ 20 ☐ 30 ☐ 45 ☐ 60+ minutes   Actual Practice: _____

WHAT YOU PRACTICED TODAY

PLAYING: ☐ New Music ☐ Repertoire ☐ Excerpt Practice ☐ Riffs & Solos ☐ Improvisation
☐ Other: _____

TECHNIQUE & SKILLS: ☐ Scales ☐ Chords ☐ Arpeggios ☐ Ear Training ☐ Exercises
☐ Rhythm & Reading ☐ Applied Theory ☐ Other: _____

CREATIVITY: ☐ Songwriting ☐ Composition ☐ Improvisation ☐ Listening & Study ☐ Lyrics
☐ Other: _____

PERFORMANCE & PROJECTS: ☐ Recording ☐ Backing Tracks ☐ Group Work ☐ Research
☐ Other: _____

TEACHER / ASSIGNMENTS / IMPROVEMENTS

_____
_____
_____
_____
_____

PROGRESS SNAPSHOT (Circle how today's practice went:)

😠   🙁   😐   🙂   😄

NEXT PRACTICE GOALS

_____
_____
_____
_____
_____

PRACTICE SESSION

DAY / DATE: _____ INSTRUMENT _____
Motivation: ☐ Low   ☐ Medium   ☐ High

TODAY'S FOCUS
1. _____
2. _____
3. _____

PRACTICE TIME
Planned: ☐ 10 ☐ 20 ☐ 30 ☐ 45 ☐ 60+ minutes   Actual Practice: _____

WHAT YOU PRACTICED TODAY

PLAYING: ☐ New Music ☐ Repertoire ☐ Excerpt Practice ☐ Riffs & Solos ☐ Improvisation
☐ Other: _____

TECHNIQUE & SKILLS: ☐ Scales ☐ Chords ☐ Arpeggios ☐ Ear Training ☐ Exercises
☐ Rhythm & Reading ☐ Applied Theory ☐ Other: _____

CREATIVITY: ☐ Songwriting ☐ Composition ☐ Improvisation ☐ Listening & Study ☐ Lyrics
☐ Other: _____

PERFORMANCE & PROJECTS: ☐ Recording ☐ Backing Tracks ☐ Group Work ☐ Research
☐ Other: _____

TEACHER / ASSIGNMENTS / IMPROVEMENTS
_____
_____
_____
_____
_____

PROGRESS SNAPSHOT (Circle how today's practice went:)

☹   😕   😐   🙂   😄

NEXT PRACTICE GOALS
_____
_____
_____

DAILY TIP:
Sound is born in silence. Claude Debussy

PRACTICE SESSION

DAY / DATE: _____ INSTRUMENT _____
Motivation: ☐ Low   ☐ Medium   ☐ High

TODAY'S FOCUS
1. _____
2. _____
3. _____

PRACTICE TIME
Planned: ☐ 10 ☐ 20 ☐ 30 ☐ 45 ☐ 60+ minutes   Actual Practice: _____

WHAT YOU PRACTICED TODAY

PLAYING: ☐ New Music ☐ Repertoire ☐ Excerpt Practice ☐ Riffs & Solos ☐ Improvisation
☐ Other: _____

TECHNIQUE & SKILLS: ☐ Scales ☐ Chords ☐ Arpeggios ☐ Ear Training ☐ Exercises
☐ Rhythm & Reading ☐ Applied Theory ☐ Other: _____

CREATIVITY: ☐ Songwriting ☐ Composition ☐ Improvisation ☐ Listening & Study ☐ Lyrics
☐ Other: _____

PERFORMANCE & PROJECTS: ☐ Recording ☐ Backing Tracks ☐ Group Work ☐ Research
☐ Other: _____

TEACHER / ASSIGNMENTS / IMPROVEMENTS
_____
_____
_____
_____
_____

PROGRESS SNAPSHOT (Circle how today's practice went:)

☹   🙁   😐   🙂   😄

NEXT PRACTICE GOALS
_____
_____
_____
_____
_____

DAY SESSION

PRACTICE SESSION

DAY / DATE: _____ INSTRUMENT _____
Motivation: ☐ Low ☐ Medium ☐ High

TODAY'S FOCUS

1. _____
2. _____
3. _____

PRACTICE TIME

Planned: ☐ 10 ☐ 20 ☐ 30 ☐ 45 ☐ 60+ minutes   Actual Practice: _____

WHAT YOU PRACTICED TODAY

PLAYING: ☐ New Music ☐ Repertoire ☐ Excerpt Practice ☐ Riffs & Solos ☐ Improvisation
☐ Other: _____

TECHNIQUE & SKILLS: ☐ Scales ☐ Chords ☐ Arpeggios ☐ Ear Training ☐ Exercises
☐ Rhythm & Reading ☐ Applied Theory ☐ Other: _____

CREATIVITY: ☐ Songwriting ☐ Composition ☐ Improvisation ☐ Listening & Study ☐ Lyrics
☐ Other: _____

PERFORMANCE & PROJECTS: ☐ Recording ☐ Backing Tracks ☐ Group Work ☐ Research
☐ Other: _____

TEACHER / ASSIGNMENTS / IMPROVEMENTS

_____
_____
_____
_____
_____

PROGRESS SNAPSHOT (Circle how today's practice went:)

☹ 🙁 😐 🙂 😊

NEXT PRACTICE GOALS

_____
_____
_____

DAILY TIP:

Notes never die; they ring forever into the universe.

PRACTICE SUMMARY

DATE RANGE: _____

TOTAL SESSIONS: _____ TOTAL TIME: _____

OVERALL FOCUS / ENERGY THIS PERIOD
☐ Strong Momentum ☐ Balanced Progress ☐ Slower Week ☐ Reset / Recovery

TOP 3 ACCOMPLISHMENTS
1. _____
2. _____
3. _____

WHAT YOU WORKED ON MOST

PLAYING: _____
_____

TECHNIQUE & SKILLS: _____
_____

CREATIVITY: _____
_____

PERFORMANCE & PROJECTS: _____
_____

DEEP PRACTICE RECAP
Piece / Exercise: _____
Current Metronome: _____ bpm   Goal: _____ bpm
Focus Area: ☐ Tone ☐ Timing ☐ Fingering ☐ Articulation ☐ Other
Improvement Plan: _____

PERFORMANCES
☐ Recorded / Video ☐ Played for Someone ☐ Ensemble /Jam ☐ None this Week

PROGRESS & INSIGHTS
What improved the most? _____
What still needs work? _____
Creative discoveries or ideas? _____

NEXT FOCUS / UPCOMING GOALS
_____
_____
_____

WEEKLY INSIGHT
Tackle the single most difficult or dreaded piece of work first thing in your practice session next week.

PRACTICE SESSION

DAY / DATE: _____ INSTRUMENT _____

Motivation: ☐ Low ☐ Medium ☐ High

TODAY'S FOCUS

1. _____
2. _____
3. _____

PRACTICE TIME

Planned: ☐ 10 ☐ 20 ☐ 30 ☐ 45 ☐ 60+ minutes   Actual Practice: _____

WHAT YOU PRACTICED TODAY

PLAYING: ☐ New Music ☐ Repertoire ☐ Excerpt Practice ☐ Riffs & Solos ☐ Improvisation
☐ Other: _____

TECHNIQUE & SKILLS: ☐ Scales ☐ Chords ☐ Arpeggios ☐ Ear Training ☐ Exercises
☐ Rhythm & Reading ☐ Applied Theory ☐ Other: _____

CREATIVITY: ☐ Songwriting ☐ Composition ☐ Improvisation ☐ Listening & Study ☐ Lyrics
☐ Other: _____

PERFORMANCE & PROJECTS: ☐ Recording ☐ Backing Tracks ☐ Group Work ☐ Research
☐ Other: _____

TEACHER / ASSIGNMENTS / IMPROVEMENTS

_____
_____
_____
_____
_____

PROGRESS SNAPSHOT (Circle how today's practice went:)

☹   🙁   😐   🙂   😊

NEXT PRACTICE GOALS

_____
_____
_____

DAILY TIP:

Listen louder than you play.

PRACTICE SESSION

DAY / DATE: _____ INSTRUMENT _____

Motivation: ☐ Low ☐ Medium ☐ High

TODAY'S FOCUS

1. _____
2. _____
3. _____

PRACTICE TIME

Planned: ☐ 10 ☐ 20 ☐ 30 ☐ 45 ☐ 60+ minutes   Actual Practice: _____

WHAT YOU PRACTICED TODAY

PLAYING: ☐ New Music ☐ Repertoire ☐ Excerpt Practice ☐ Riffs & Solos ☐ Improvisation
☐ Other: _____

TECHNIQUE & SKILLS: ☐ Scales ☐ Chords ☐ Arpeggios ☐ Ear Training ☐ Exercises
☐ Rhythm & Reading ☐ Applied Theory ☐ Other: _____

CREATIVITY: ☐ Songwriting ☐ Composition ☐ Improvisation ☐ Listening & Study ☐ Lyrics
☐ Other: _____

PERFORMANCE & PROJECTS: ☐ Recording ☐ Backing Tracks ☐ Group Work ☐ Research
☐ Other: _____

TEACHER / ASSIGNMENTS / IMPROVEMENTS

_____
_____
_____
_____
_____

PROGRESS SNAPSHOT (Circle how today's practice went:)

😠 ☹ 😐 🙂 😄

NEXT PRACTICE GOALS

_____
_____
_____
_____
_____

DAY SESSION

PRACTICE SESSION

DAY / DATE: _____ INSTRUMENT _____
Motivation: ☐ Low ☐ Medium ☐ High

TODAY'S FOCUS

1. _____
2. _____
3. _____

PRACTICE TIME

Planned: ☐ 10 ☐ 20 ☐ 30 ☐ 45 ☐ 60+ minutes   Actual Practice: _____

WHAT YOU PRACTICED TODAY

PLAYING: ☐ New Music ☐ Repertoire ☐ Excerpt Practice ☐ Riffs & Solos ☐ Improvisation
☐ Other: _____

TECHNIQUE & SKILLS: ☐ Scales ☐ Chords ☐ Arpeggios ☐ Ear Training ☐ Exercises
☐ Rhythm & Reading ☐ Applied Theory ☐ Other: _____

CREATIVITY: ☐ Songwriting ☐ Composition ☐ Improvisation ☐ Listening & Study ☐ Lyrics
☐ Other: _____

PERFORMANCE & PROJECTS: ☐ Recording ☐ Backing Tracks ☐ Group Work ☐ Research
☐ Other: _____

TEACHER / ASSIGNMENTS / IMPROVEMENTS

_____
_____
_____
_____
_____

PROGRESS SNAPSHOT (Circle how today's practice went:)

☹ 🙁 😐 🙂 😄

NEXT PRACTICE GOALS

_____
_____
_____

DAILY TIP:

Hear the note before you play it.

PRACTICE SESSION

DAY / DATE: _____ INSTRUMENT _____
Motivation: ☐ Low ☐ Medium ☐ High

TODAY'S FOCUS
1. _____
2. _____
3. _____

PRACTICE TIME
Planned: ☐ 10 ☐ 20 ☐ 30 ☐ 45 ☐ 60+ minutes   Actual Practice: _____

WHAT YOU PRACTICED TODAY

PLAYING: ☐ New Music ☐ Repertoire ☐ Excerpt Practice ☐ Riffs & Solos ☐ Improvisation
☐ Other: _____

TECHNIQUE & SKILLS: ☐ Scales ☐ Chords ☐ Arpeggios ☐ Ear Training ☐ Exercises
☐ Rhythm & Reading ☐ Applied Theory ☐ Other: _____

CREATIVITY: ☐ Songwriting ☐ Composition ☐ Improvisation ☐ Listening & Study ☐ Lyrics
☐ Other: _____

PERFORMANCE & PROJECTS: ☐ Recording ☐ Backing Tracks ☐ Group Work ☐ Research
☐ Other: _____

TEACHER / ASSIGNMENTS / IMPROVEMENTS
_____
_____
_____
_____
_____

PROGRESS SNAPSHOT (Circle how today's practice went:)

😠 ☹ 😐 🙂 😊

NEXT PRACTICE GOALS
_____
_____
_____
_____
_____

DAY SESSION

PRACTICE SESSION

DAY / DATE: _____ INSTRUMENT _____
Motivation: ☐ Low   ☐ Medium   ☐ High

TODAY'S FOCUS
1. _____
2. _____
3. _____

PRACTICE TIME
Planned: ☐ 10 ☐ 20 ☐ 30 ☐ 45 ☐ 60+ minutes   Actual Practice: _____

WHAT YOU PRACTICED TODAY

PLAYING: ☐ New Music ☐ Repertoire ☐ Excerpt Practice ☐ Riffs & Solos ☐ Improvisation
☐ Other: _____

TECHNIQUE & SKILLS: ☐ Scales ☐ Chords ☐ Arpeggios ☐ Ear Training ☐ Exercises
☐ Rhythm & Reading ☐ Applied Theory ☐ Other: _____

CREATIVITY: ☐ Songwriting ☐ Composition ☐ Improvisation ☐ Listening & Study ☐ Lyrics
☐ Other: _____

PERFORMANCE & PROJECTS: ☐ Recording ☐ Backing Tracks ☐ Group Work ☐ Research
☐ Other: _____

TEACHER / ASSIGNMENTS / IMPROVEMENTS
_____
_____
_____
_____
_____

PROGRESS SNAPSHOT (Circle how today's practice went:)

😠   🙁   😐   🙂   😊

NEXT PRACTICE GOALS
_____
_____
_____

DAILY TIP:
Make haste slowly. Beethoven

PRACTICE SUMMARY

DATE RANGE: _____
TOTAL SESSIONS: _____ TOTAL TIME: _____

OVERALL FOCUS / ENERGY THIS PERIOD
☐ Strong Momentum ☐ Balanced Progress ☐ Slower Week ☐ Reset / Recovery

TOP 3 ACCOMPLISHMENTS
1. _____
2. _____
3. _____

WHAT YOU WORKED ON MOST

PLAYING: _____
_____

TECHNIQUE & SKILLS: _____
_____

CREATIVITY: _____
_____

PERFORMANCE & PROJECTS: _____
_____

DEEP PRACTICE RECAP
Piece / Exercise: _____
Current Metronome: _____ bpm   Goal: _____ bpm
Focus Area: ☐ Tone ☐ Timing ☐ Fingering ☐ Articulation ☐ Other
Improvement Plan: _____

PERFORMANCES
☐ Recorded / Video ☐ Played for Someone ☐ Ensemble / Jam ☐ None this Week

PROGRESS & INSIGHTS
What improved the most? _____
What still needs work? _____
Creative discoveries or ideas? _____

NEXT FOCUS / UPCOMING GOALS
_____
_____
_____

WEEKLY INSIGHT
Begin with listening; it is your first instrument.

TEACHER / LESSON NOTES

LESSON DATE: _____ INSTRUMENT _____
Readiness: ☐ Low   ☐ Medium   ☐ High

ASSIGNMENTS / FOCUS POINTS
1. _____
2. _____
3. _____
4. _____
5. _____

HOW LONG YOU SHOULD PRACTICE AT EACH SESSION
Planned: ☐ 10   ☐ 20   ☐ 30   ☐ 45   ☐ 60+ minutes   Other: _____

TECHNIQUE & SKILLS: ☐ Scales   ☐ Chords   ☐ Arpeggios   ☐ Ear Training   ☐ Exercises
☐ Rhythm & Reading   ☐ Applied Theory   ☐ Other: _____
_____
_____

REPERTOIRE 1
Title / Section: _____
Measures / Focus: _____   Tempo Goal: _____ bpm

REPERTOIRE 2
Title / Section: _____
Measures / Focus: _____   Tempo Goal: _____ bpm

REPERTOIRE 3
Title / Section: _____
Measures / Focus: _____   Tempo Goal: _____ bpm

TEACHER COMMENTS
_____
_____
_____
_____
_____

STUDENT NOTES
_____
_____
_____

IDEAS & NOTES

MONTHLY REFLECTION

MONTH: _____ TOTAL TIME: _____
TOTAL SESSIONS: _____ TOTAL PERFORMANCES: _____

RATE YOUR PROGRESS THIS MONTH: BELOW ★   AVERAGE ★ ★   ABOVE ★ ★ ★

WHAT ARE YOU MOST GRATEFUL FOR WITH YOUR MUSIC THIS MONTH

_____
_____
_____
_____
_____

SET YOUR GOALS FOR NEXT MONTH

_____
_____
_____
_____
_____

POSITIVE LESSONS OR HABITS TO CONTINUE NEXT MONTH

_____
_____
_____
_____
_____

NOTES

_____
_____
_____
_____

INSIGHT

Measure this month's success by what you learned, not what you finished.

SEASON REVIEW

Review Period: _____

Completion Date: _____

Total Practice Hours (Approx.): _____

Key Accomplishments:
_____
_____
_____
_____
_____

Areas of Future Focus:
_____
_____
_____
_____
_____

Next 12-Month Musical Goal:
_____
_____
_____
_____
_____

The value of a practice is not measured by its length, but by its result.

Integrated Theory and Reference Section

The Theory & Reference section is designed to be a quick-check resource you can use while practicing, composing or preparing for a gig.

The following charts are more for reference and quick recall than a complete, comprehensive course on music theory. If you are looking for in-depth lessons, tutorials, and more information about music theory, please check the dedicated resources on the Kalymi Music Publishing website.

THEORY & REFERENCE TABLE OF CONTENTS

Key Signatures 210

Circle of Fifths..211

Chord Formulas & Spelling Guide...212

Major & Minor Inversions 214

Master Reference Scale Chart 215

Mode Reference Guide 216

Improvisation Map 217

Interval & Keyboard Charts 218

Figured Bass & Nashville Number System....................................219

Instrument Ranges 220

Standard Transposing Instrument Reference Chart........................221

Time Signatures & Rhythm Charts 222

Major & Minor Key Signatures

The major and relative minor key signatures in treble and bass clef.

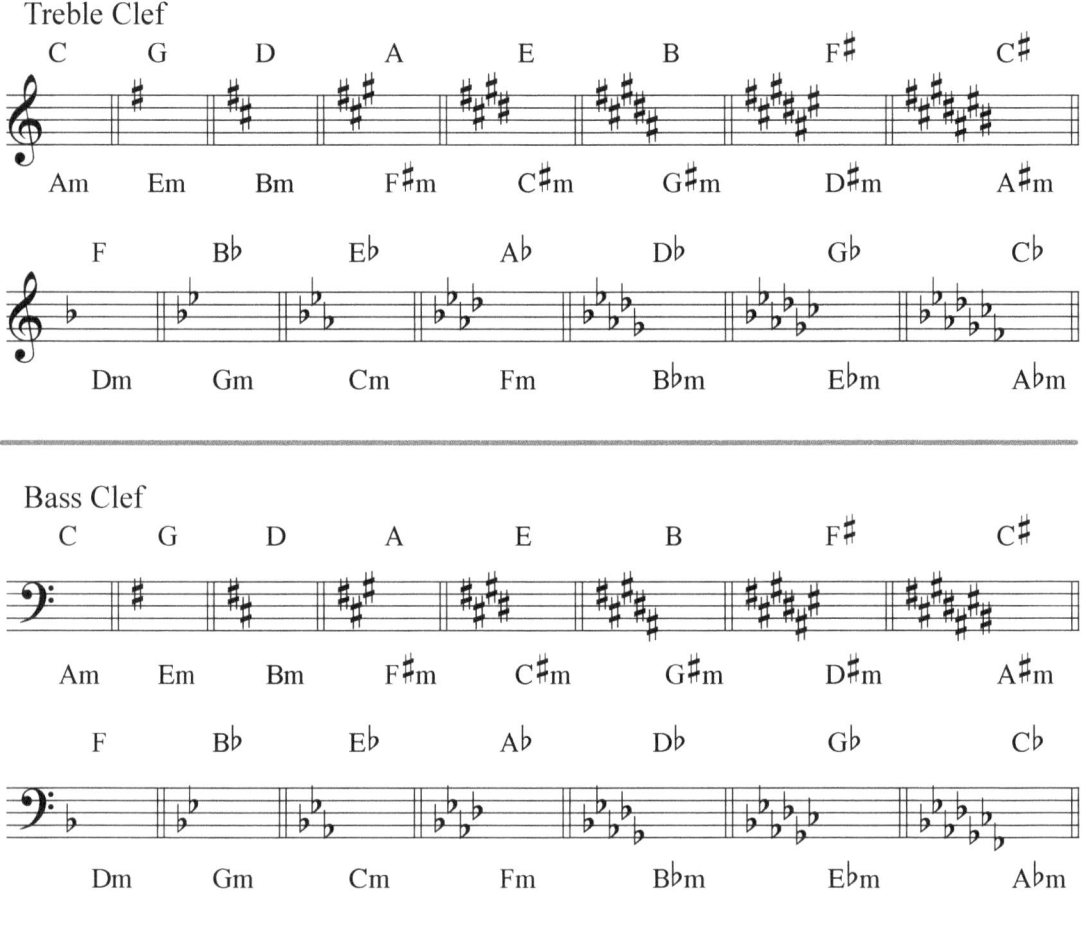

Order of Sharps and Flats

"Father Charles Goes Down And Ends Battle" is a mnemonic that shows the order of sharps, and reversed, gives the order of flats in key signatures: ***Battle Ends And Down Goes Charles Father.***

	Sharps ♯	Key
Father	F♯	G
Charles	F♯C♯	D
Goes	F♯C♯G♯	A
Down	F♯C♯G♯D♯	E
And	F♯C♯G♯D♯A♯	B
Ends	F♯C♯G♯D♯A♯E♯	F♯
Battle	F♯C♯G♯D♯A♯E♯B♯	C♯

	Flats ♭	Key
Battle	B♭	F
Ends	B♭E♭	B♭
And	B♭E♭A♭	E♭
Down	B♭E♭A♭D♭	A♭
Goes	B♭E♭A♭D♭G♭	D♭
Charles	B♭E♭A♭D♭G♭C♭	G♭
Father	B♭E♭A♭D♭G♭C♭F♭	C♭

Circle of Fifths & Fourths

The circle of fifths and fourths is one of the most informative charts a musician can have. If you read clockwise, the notes are a perfect fifth apart (5th), while counter-clockwise shows the notes a perfect fourth apart (4th).

The small circled number on the outer edge shows how many sharps or flats are in a key, the larger letter is the major key, the two chords below the major keys show the iim-V7 for each key, and the colored inner circle shows the relative minor key.

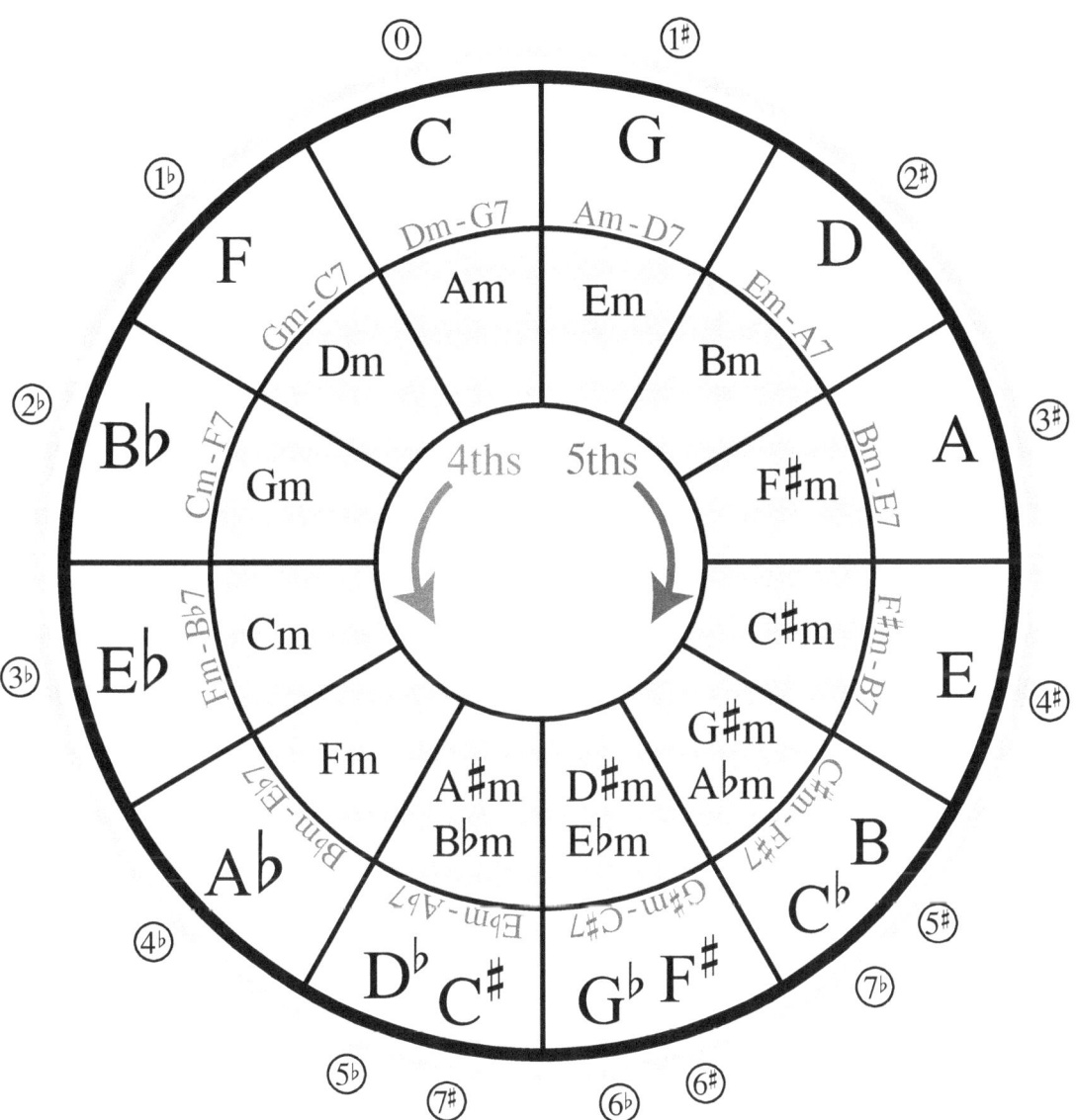

Chord Formulas & Spelling Guide

Every chord comes from a scale. Each note in that scale has a degree number: C=1, D=2, E=3, and so on. Chord formulas use these scale degrees to show which notes form the chord. For example, the numbers below represent the scale degrees of the C major scale.

C	D	E	F	G	A	B	C	D	E	F	G	A
1	2	3	4	5	6	7	8	9	10	11	12	13

The chart below lists the exact notes that make up the three most common chord types: major, minor, and dominant seventh.

MAJOR (1 3 5)

Root	1	3	5
A	A	C♯	E
A♯	A♯	C𝄪	E♯
B♭	B♭	D	F
B	B	D♯	F♯
C	C	E	G
C♯	C♯	E♯	G♯
D♭	D♭	F	A♭
D	D	F♯	A
D♯	D♯	F𝄪	A♯
E♭	E♭	G	B♭
E	E	G♯	B
F	F	A	C
F♯	F♯	A♯	C♯
G♭	G♭	B♭	D♭
G	G	B	D
A♭	A♭	C	E♭

MINOR (1 ♭3 5)

Root	1	♭3	5
Am	A	C	E
A♯m	A♯	C♯	E♯
B♭m	B♭	D♭	F
Bm	B	D	F♯
Cm	C	E♭	G
C♯m	C♯	E	G♯
D♭m	D♭	F♭	A♭
Dm	D	F	A
D♯m	D♯	F♯	A♯
E♭m	E♭	G♭	B♭
Em	E	G	B
Fm	F	A♭	C
F♯m	F♯	A	C♯
G♭m	G♭	B♭♭	D♭
Gm	G	B♭	D
A♭m	A♭	C♭	E♭

DOMINANT 7th (1 3 5 ♭7)

Root	1	3	5	♭7
A7	A	C♯	E	G
A♯7	A♯	C𝄪	E♯	G♯
B♭7	B♭	D	F	A♭
B7	B	D♯	F♯	A
C7	C	E	G	B♭
C♯7	C♯	E♯	G♯	B
D♭7	D♭	F	A♭	C♭
D7	D	F♯	A	C
D♯7	D♯	F𝄪	A♯	C♯
E♭7	E♭	G	B♭	D♭
E7	E	G♯	B	D
F7	F	A	C	E♭
F♯7	F♯	A♯	C♯	E
G♭7	G♭	B♭	D♭	F♭
G7	G	B	D	F
A♭7	A♭	C	E♭	G♭

This comprehensive chart summarizes the formulas and scale degrees for the most common chord types in modern music. Each entry shows the scale-degree pattern used to build the chord so you can spell it correctly in any key.

MAJOR CHORDS

NAME	ABBREVIATION	SCALE DEGREES
major	Usually none or capital M	1 3 5
power chord	5	1 5
major sixth	6	1 3 5 6
major seventh	maj7	1 3 5 7
major ninth	maj9	1 3 5 7 9

Major seventh sharp five	maj7♯5	1 3 ♯5 7
major sixth ninth	6/9	1 3 5 6 9
major seventh sharp eleven	Maj7♯11	1 3 5 7 (9)* ♯11 *(optional)

MINOR CHORDS

NAME	ABBREVIATION	CHORD TONES
minor	m	1 ♭3 5
minor sixth	m6	1 ♭3 5 6
minor seventh	m7	1 ♭3 5 ♭7
minor major seventh	m/maj7	1 ♭3 5 7
minor seventh flat 5	m7♭5 (half diminished)	1 ♭3 ♭5 ♭7
minor ninth	m9	1 ♭3 (5) ♭7 9
minor eleventh	m11	1 ♭3 (5) ♭7 (9) 11
minor thirteenth	M13	1 ♭3 (5) ♭7 (9) 11 13

DOMINANT CHORDS

NAME	ABBREVIATION	CHORD TONES
Dom. seventh	7, dom7	1 3 5 ♭7
Dom. ninth	9	1 3 5 ♭7 9
Dom. thirteenth	13	1 3 5 ♭7 9 13
Dom. seventh flat 5	7♭5	1 3 ♭5 ♭7
Dom. seventh sharp 5	7♯5	1 3 ♯5 ♭7
Dom. seventh flat 9	7♭9	1 3 (5) ♭7 ♭9
Dom. seventh sharp 9	7♯9	1 3 (5) ♭7 ♯9
Dom. thirteenth flat 9	13♭9	1 3 (5) ♭7 ♭9 13

SUSPENDED - ADD CHORDS

NAME	ABBREVIATION	CHORD TONES
Suspended 2nd	sus2	1 2 5
suspended 4th	sus4	1 4 5
Dom. 7 suspended 4th	7sus4	1 4 5 ♭7
Dom. 9 suspended 4th	9sus4	1 4 (5) ♭7 9
Add two	add2	1 2 3 5
Add nine	add9	1 3 5 9
Minor add nine	m(add9)	1 ♭3 5 9

DIMINISHED - AUGMENTED CHORDS

NAME	ABBREVIATION	CHORD TONES
diminished	dim, °	1 ♭3 ♭5
diminished seventh	dim7, °7	1 ♭3 ♭5 ♭♭7
augmented	aug, +	1 3 ♯5
augmented seventh	aug7, +7	1 3 ♯5 7

Major and Minor Chord Inversions Chart

This chart is an Inversion Reference Guide that shows the exact note order for major and minor triads in all 12 keys in root position, first inversion, and second inversion.

Major Chord	Root Position	1st Inversion	2nd Inversion	Minor Chord	Root Position	1st Inversion	2nd Inversion
F	F A C	A C F	C F A	Fm	F A♭ C	A♭ C F	C F A♭
C	C E G	E G C	G C E	Cm	C E♭ G	E♭ G C	G C E♭
G	G B D	B D G	D G B	Gm	G B♭ D	B♭ D G	D G B♭
D	D F♯ A	F♯ A D	A D F♯	Dm	D F A	F A D	A D F
A	A C♯ E	C♯ E A	E A C♯	Am	A C E	C E A	E A C
E	E G♯ B	G♯ B E	B E G♯	Em	E G B	G B E	B E G
B	B D♯ F♯	D♯ F♯ B	F♯ B D♯	Bm	B D F♯	D F♯ B	F♯ B D
B♭	B♭ D F	D F B♭	F B♭ D	B♭m	B♭ D♭ F	D♭ F B♭	F B♭ D♭
E♭	E♭ G B♭	G B♭ E♭	B♭ E♭ G	E♭m	E♭ G♭ B♭	G♭ B♭ E♭	B♭ E♭ G♭
A♭	A♭ C E♭	C E♭ A♭	E♭ A♭ C	A♭m	A♭ C♭ E♭	C♭ E♭ A♭	E♭ A♭ C♭
D♭	D♭ F A♭	F A♭ D♭	A♭ D♭ F	D♭m	D♭ F♭ A♭	F♭ A♭ D♭	A♭ D♭ F♭
G♭	G♭ B♭ D♭	B♭ D♭ G♭	D♭ G♭ B♭	G♭m	G♭ B♭♭ D♭	B♭♭ D♭ G♭	D♭ G♭ B♭♭
C♭	C♭ E♭ G♭	E♭ G♭ C♭	G♭ C♭ E♭	C♭m	C♭ E♭♭ G♭	E♭♭ G♭ C♭	G♭ C♭ E♭♭
F♯	F♯ A♯ C♯	A♯ C♯ F♯	C♯ F♯ A♯	F♯m	F♯ A C♯	A C♯ F♯	C♯ F♯ A
C♯	C♯ E♯ G♯	E♯ G♯ C♯	G♯ C♯ E♯	C♯m	C♯ E G♯	E G♯ C♯	G♯ C♯ E
G♯	G♯ B♯ D♯	B♯ D♯ G♯	D♯ G♯ B♯	G♯m	G♯ B D♯	B D♯ G♯	D♯ G♯ B
D♯	D♯ F♯ A♯	F♯ A♯ D♯	A♯ D♯ F♯	D♯m	D♯ F♯ A♯	F♯ A♯ D♯	A♯ D♯ F♯
A♯	A♯ C♯ E♯	C♯ E♯ A♯	E♯ A♯ C♯	A♯m	A♯ C♯ E♯	C♯ E♯ A♯	E♯ A♯ C♯

Master Reference Scale Chart

This comprehensive chart details the structures, scale degrees, and notes for 25 essential scales across classical, jazz, symmetrical, and world music systems, all built from the tonic note C.

Group	Scale Name	Scale Degrees	Notes (Starting on C)
Diatonic	Major (Ionian)	1-2-3-4-5-6-7	C-D-E-F-G-A-B
Diatonic	Natural Minor (Aeolian)	1-2-♭3-4-5-♭6-♭7	C-D-E♭-F-G-A♭-B♭
Diatonic	Dorian Mode	1-2-♭3-4-5-6-♭7	C-D-E♭-F-G-A-B♭
Diatonic	Lydian Mode	1-2-3-♯4-5-6-7	C-D-E-F♯-G-A-B
Diatonic	Mixolydian Mode	1-2-3-4-5-6-♭7	C-D-E-F-G-A-B♭
Diatonic	Phrygian Mode	1-♭2-♭3-4-5-♭6-♭7	C-D♭-E♭-F-G-A♭-B♭
Diatonic	Locrian Mode	1-♭2-♭3-4-♭5-♭6-♭7	C-D♭-E♭-F-G♭-A♭-B♭
Minor Variants	Harmonic Minor	1-2-♭3-4-5-♭6-7	C-D-E♭-F-G-A♭-B
Minor Variants	Melodic Minor (Asc.)	1-2-♭3-4-5-6-7	C-D-E♭-F-G-A-B
Pentatonic	Major Pentatonic	1-2-3-5-6	C-D-E-G-A
Pentatonic	Minor Pentatonic	1-♭3-4-5-♭7	C-E♭-F-G-B♭
Blues	Minor Blues Scale	1-♭3-4-♯4-5-♭7	C-E♭-F-F♯-G-B♭
Blues	Major Blues Scale	1-2-♭3-3-5-6	C-D-E♭-E-G-A
Symmetrical	Whole Tone Scale	1-2-3-♯4-♯5-♯6	C-D-E-F♯-G♯-A♯
Symmetrical	Diminished (Half-Whole)	1-♭2-♭3-3-♭5-5-6-♭7	C-D♭-E♭-E-G♭-G-A-B♭
Symmetrical	Diminished (Whole-Half)	1-2-♭3-4-♭5-♭6-6-7	C-D-E♭-F-G♭-A♭-A-B
Symmetrical	Augmented Scale	1-♭3-3-5-♯5-7	C-E♭-E-G-G♯-B
Exotic/World	Phrygian Dominant	1-♭2-3-4-5-♭6-♭7	C-D♭-E-F-G-A♭-B♭
Exotic/World	Double Harmonic Major	1-♭2-3-4-5-♭6-7	C-D♭-E-F-G-A♭-B
Exotic/World	Hungarian Minor	1-2-♭3-♯4-5-♭6-7	C-D-E♭-F♯-G-A♭-B
Jazz	Altered (Super Locrian)	1-♭2-♭3-♭4-♭5-♭6-♭7	C-D♭-E♭-E-G♭-A♭-B♭
Jazz	Lydian Dominant	1-2-3-♯4-5-6-♭7	C-D-E-F♯-G-A-B♭
Jazz	Bebop Major	1-2-3-4-5-♯5-6-7	C-D-E-F-G-G♯-A-B
Jazz	Bebop Dominant	1-2-3-4-5-♯5-♭7-7	C-D-E-F-G-G♯-B♭-B
Foundational	Chromatic Scale	1-♭2-2-♭3-3-4-♭5-5-♭6-6-♭7-7	C-D♭-D-E♭-E-F-G♭-G-A♭-A-B♭-B

Mode Reference Guide

The mode is a type of scale that can be understood in two ways: as a variation of the major scale or as its own key center with a tonic.

In the diagram below, the mode name appears outside the circle, and the outer circle shows the scale notes that form the mode. For example, the scale notes for the Ionian mode are: 1-2-3-4-5-6-7. The second outer ring shows the scale degrees that make the mode unique. For example, the Lydian mode has a ♯4 and a natural 7th. Two of the modes are exactly like our major (Ionian) and natural minor scale (Aeolian). The center of the circle shows the modes in relation to the major key. For example, in the key of C, Ionian is mode 1, Dorian 2, Phrygian 3, Lydian 4, Mixolydian 5, Aeolian 6, and Locrian 7.

Modes are essential for understanding improvisation and a very useful tool for composition.

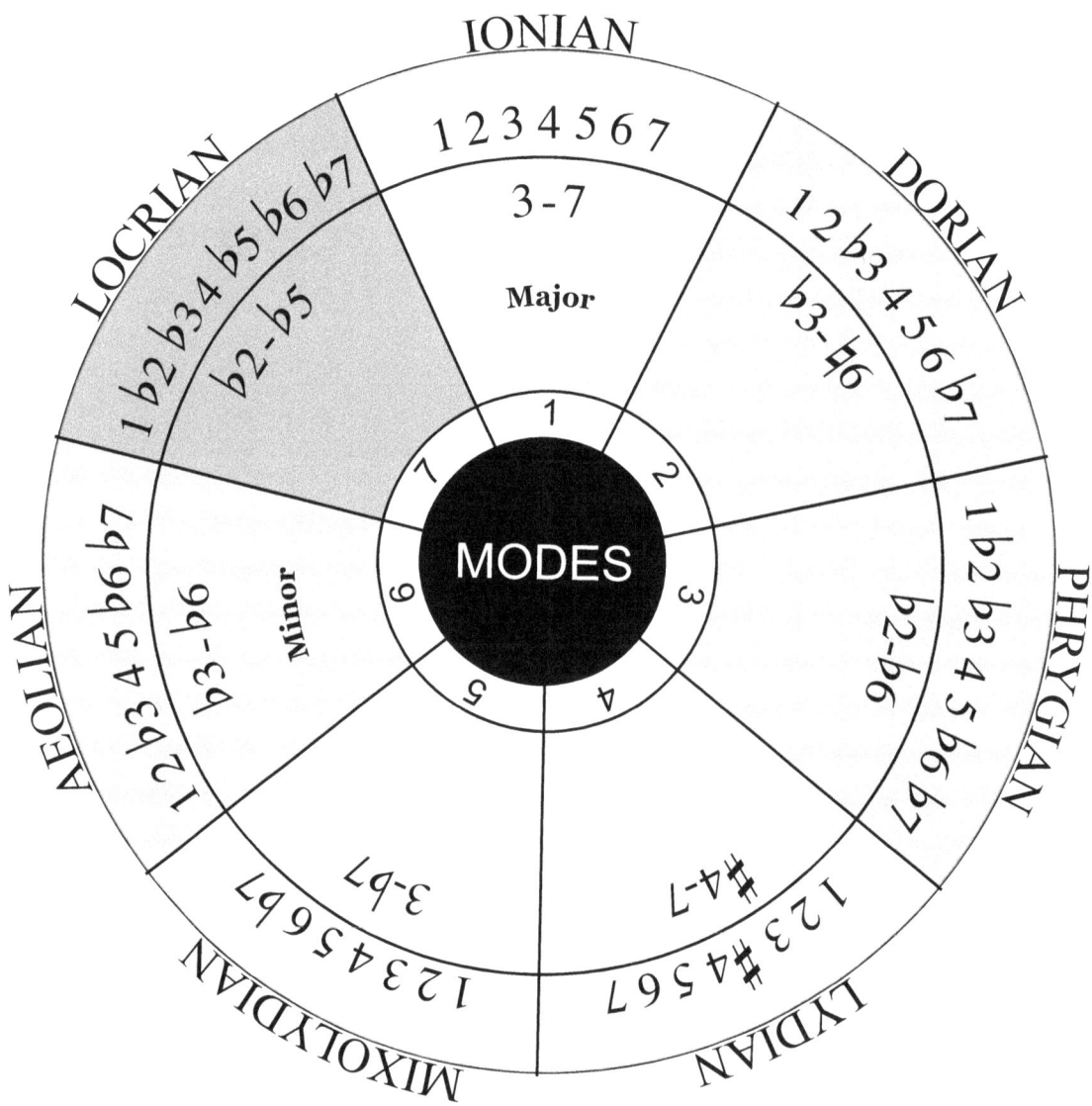

Mode Memory Tip:

MODES	Ionian	Dorian	Phrygian	Lydian	Mixolydian	Aeolian	Locrian
Mnemonic	I	Don't	Play	Like	My	Aunt	Lucy

Improvisation Chord & Scale Reference

Use this generalized Improvisation Chart to find scales that fit each chord when you are soloing or composing. Start with the primary scale for a traditional approach, then try the secondary scale to add color or tension. For example, if you have a CMaj7 chord, then you can play the primary Ionian (major) scale or the Lydian mode as the secondary choice.

Chord	Scale (Primary)	Scale (Secondary)
Maj7	Ionian	Lydian
Maj6/9	Ionian	Lydian
Maj7♯11	Lydian	Lydian Aug
maj7♯5	Lydian Aug	Whole-tone
m7	Dorian	Aeolian
m6	Dorian	Melodic Minor
m7(♭6)	Aeolian	Dorian
mMaj7	Melodic Minor	Harm. Minor
m7♭5 (half-dim)	Locrian nat2 (m-mode-2)	Locrian
dim7	Whole-Half Dim.	Harm. Minor
7	Mixolydian	Mixolydian ♭9 ♭13
7(♭9)	Half-Whole Dim.	Altered
7(♯9)	Altered	Half-Whole Dim.
7(♭13)	Mixolydian ♭6	Altered
7(♯11)	Lydian Dominant	Mixolydian
7sus4	Mixolydian	Dorian
7alt	Altered (mm7)	Half-Whole Dim.
7♭9♯11	Half-Whole Dim.	Altered
7 (V of i)	Altered	H-W Dim.
7 (V of i)	Phrygian Dom (h-mode-5)	Altered
Blues I (Tonic)	Minor Blues	Major Blues
Blues IV (Subdominant)	Minor Pentatonic + ♭5	Mixolydian
Blues V (Dominant)	Mixolydian	Altered

Interval Reference Charts & Keyboards

Semitones	Interval	Note Pair	Enharmonic
0	PU (Perfect unison)	C - C	
1	m2 (minor 2nd)	C - Db	C - C# (aug Unison)
2	M2 (Major 2nd)	C - D	C - Ebb (dim.3rd)
3	m3 (minor 3rd)	C - Eb	C - D# (aug 2nd)
4	M3 (Major 3rd)	C - E	C - Fb (dim.4th)
5	P4 (Perfect 4th)	C - F	C - E# (aug 3rd)
6	x4 / °5 (aug. 4th) (dim. 5th)	C - F#/Gb	(Tritone)
7	P5 (Perfect 5th)	C - G	
8	m6 (minor 6th)	C - Ab	C - G# (aug 5th)
9	M6 (major 6th)	C - A	C - Bbb (dim 7th)
10	m7 (minor 7th)	C - Bb	C - A# (aug 6th)
11	M7 (Major 7th)	C - B	C - Cb (dim 8th)
12	P8 (Perfect Octave)	C - C	
13	m9 (minor 9th)	C - Db	C - C# (aug 8th)
14	M9 (Major 9)	C - D	
15	m10 (minor 10th)	C - Eb	
16	M10 (Major 10th)	C - E	
17	P11 (Perfect 11th)	C - F	
18	x11 / °12 (aug. 11th) (dim. 12th)	C - F#/Gb	(Tritone)
19	P12 (Perfect 12th)	C - G	
20	m13 (minor 13th)	C - Ab	
21	M13 (Major 13th)	C - A	

Interval Matrix

NOTE	C	C#/Db	D	D#/Eb	E	F	F#/Gb	G	G#/Ab	A	A#/Bb	B
C	PU	m2	M2	m3	M3	P4	+4/°5	P5	m6	M6	m7	M7
C#/Db	M7	PU	m2	M2	m3	M3	P4	+4/°5	P5	m6	M6	m7
D	m7	M7	PU	m2	M2	m3	M3	P4	+4/°5	P5	m6	M6
D#/Eb	M6	m7	M7	PU	m2	M2	m3	M3	P4	+4/°5	P5	m6
E	m6	M6	m7	M7	PU	m2	M2	m3	M3	P4	+4/°5	P5
F	P5	m6	M6	m7	M7	PU	m2	M2	m3	M3	P4	+4/°5
F#/Gb	+4/°5	P5	m6	M6	m7	M7	PU	m2	M2	m3	M3	P4
G	P4	+4/°5	P5	m6	M6	m7	M7	PU	m2	M2	m3	M3
G#/Ab	M3	P4	+4/°5	P5	m6	M6	m7	M7	PU	m2	M2	m3
A	m3	M3	P4	+4/°5	P5	m6	M6	m7	M7	PU	m2	M2
A#/Bb	M2	m3	M3	P4	+4/°5	P5	m6	M6	m7	M7	PU	m2
B	m2	M2	m3	M3	P4	+4/°5	P5	m6	M6	m7	M7	PU

Figured Bass & Nashville Number System Reference

A quick reference that shows each chord's harmonic function written in different systems based in the key of C: Roman numeral, figured bass, Nashville number, and chord symbol.

Chord Function	Roman Numeral	Figured Bass	Nashville Number	Chord Symbol
Major (Tonic)	I	5/3	1	C (root)
1st inversion	I^6	6/3	1/3	C/E
2nd inversion	I$^6_4$	6/4	1/5	C/G
Minor	i	5/3	1m	Cm
Diminished	vii°	♭5/3	7°	Bdim/B°
Augmented	I$^+$	+5/3	1$^+$	Caug/ C+
Dominant (Major)	V	5/3	5	G
Dominant 7th	V^7	7/5/3	5^7/3	G7/B
Dominant 9th	V9	9	59	G9
Dominant 7♭9	V7♭9	♭9	57♭9	G7♭9
1st inversion (7th)	V$^6_5$	6/5	5^7/3	G7/B
2nd inversion (7th)	V$^4_3$	4/3	5^7/5	G7/D
3rd inversion (7th)	V$^4_2$	4/2	5^7/7	G7/F
Subdominant	IV	5/3	4	F
Minor Subdominant	iv	5/3	4m	Fm
Supertonic	ii	5/3	2m	Dm
Leading Tone (Diminished)	vii°	♭5/3	7°	Bdim7/B°7
Half-Diminished 7th	viiø^7	♭7,♭5	7m7♭5	Bm7♭5 or Bø^7
Major 7th	IM^7	M7	1△	Cmaj7, C△
Minor 7th	ii^7, iii^7, vi^7	7	2^7, 3^7, 6^7	Dm7, Em7, Am7
Suspended 4th	Vsus4	4/3 (4-3)	5sus4	Gsus4
Suspended 2nd	—	(2-1)	5sus2	Gsus2
Add 6th	I^6	6	1^6	C6
Add 9th / 2nd	—	—	1add9 / 1add2	Cadd9
Italian Augmented 6th	It^6	6/3	♭6 $^{6/3}$	A♭CF♯
French Augmented 6th	Fr^6	6/4/3	♭6 $^{6/4/3}$	A♭CDF♯
German Augmented 6th	Ger^6	6/5/3	♭6 $^{6/5/3}$	A♭CE♭F♯

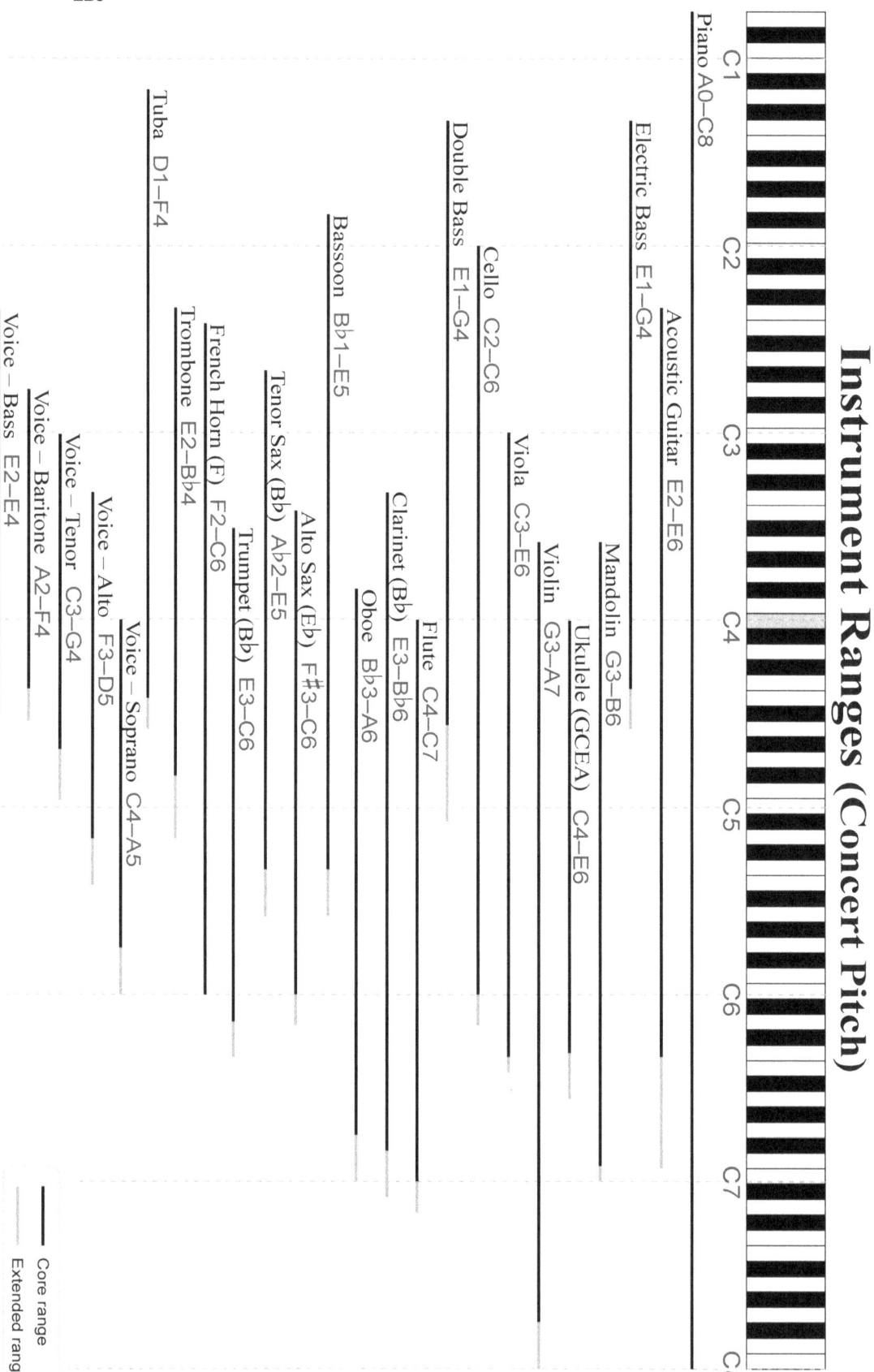

Standard Transposing Instrument Reference Chart

To use this chart, find your instrument in the first column. The middle column tells you exactly what note you read and what pitch you actually hear (**Written → Sound**). The final column (**Interval**) gives you the precise number of half-steps you need to count up or down to quickly translate your part to the true concert pitch.

INSTRUMENT	WRITTEN → SOUND	INTERVAL
Non-Transposing Instruments (Pitch Class C)	C → C	0
Flute, Oboe, Violin, Trombone, Piano, Tuba, Bassoon, Harp, Marimba, Vibraphone	C → C	0
Octave Transposing (High)		
Piccolo, Xylophone, Celesta	C → C (8va)	+12
Glockenspiel	C → C (15ma)	+24
Octave Transposing (Low)		
Guitar, Electric Bass, Double Bass	C → C (8vb)	-12
Transposing Up a Minor Third (E♭)		
Clarinet (E♭)	C → E♭	+3
Transposing Down a Major Second (B♭)		
Clarinet (B♭), Trumpet (B♭), Soprano Sax	C → B♭	-2
Tenor Sax, Bass Clarinet (B♭)	C → B♭ (8vb)	-14
Contrabass Clarinet	C → B♭ (15vb)	-26
Transposing Down a Major Sixth (E♭)		
Alto Sax (E♭), Alto Clarinet (E♭)	C → E♭	-9
Baritone Sax (E♭)	C → E♭ (8vb)	-21
Transposing Down a Perfect Fourth (F)		
French Horn (F), English Horn, Bassett Horn	C → F	-7
Transposing Down a Minor Third (A)		
Clarinet (A), Trumpet (A), Oboe d'amore	C → A	-3
Transposing Up a Major Second (D)		
D Trumpet, Clarinet (D)	C → D	+2

Time Signature & Rhythm Charts

The top note shows the beats in a measure.
The bottom note is the pulse subdivision.

Simple Duple Time   Simple Triple Time   Simple Quadruple Time

*¢ = 2/2 Cut Time (alla breve)   *C = 4/4 Common Time

Compound Duple Time   Compound Triple Time   Compound Quadruple Time

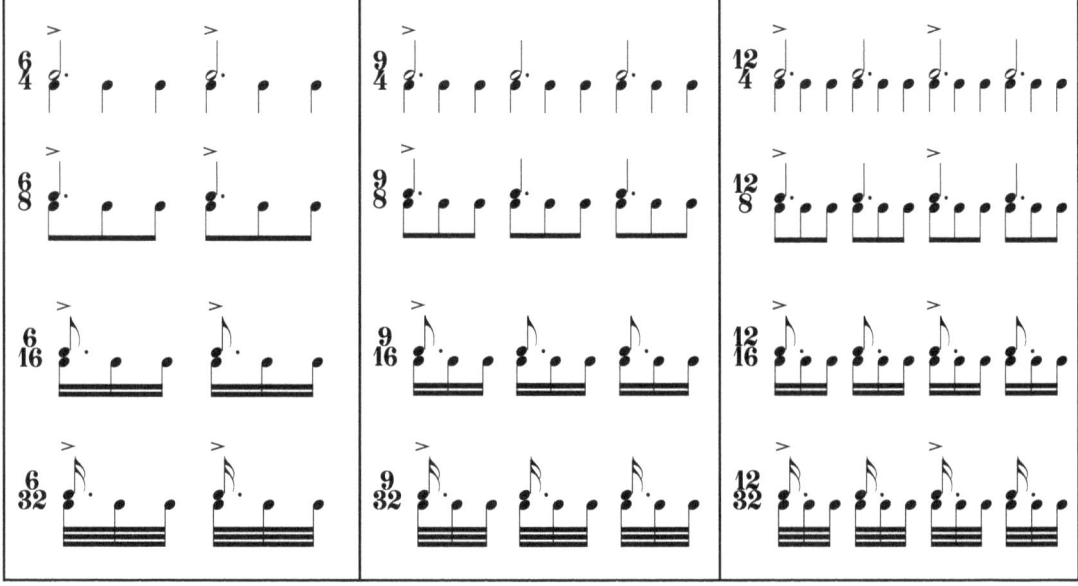

Irregular & Asymmetrical Time Signatures

Irregular Time Signatures			Additive Grouping Examples
5/4	5/8	5/16	(2+3) (3+2)
7/4	7/8	7/16	(2+2+3) (3+2+2) (2+3+2)
8/4	8/8	8/16	(3+3+2) (2+3+3) (3+2+3)
10/4	10/8	10/16	(3+3+2+2) (2+2+3+3) (3+2+2+3)
11/4	11/8	11/16	(3+3+3+2) (4+4+3) (3+2+2+4)
13/4	13/8	13/16	(3+3+2+2+3) (3+2+2+3+2+1)
15/4	15/8	15/16	(2+2+3+3+5) (3+2+2+3+2+3)

Mixed Meter & Polyrhythmic

Mixed Meter

Mixed Meter	Beats
3/4 + 4/4	7 x ♩
4/4 + 3/4	7 x ♩
2/4 + 3/4	5 x ♩
3/4 + 2/4 + 2/4	7 x ♩
6/8 + 4/4	10 x ♪
5/8 + 3/8	8 x ♪

Polyrhythms

3:2	(2/4)
4:3	(3/4)
5:4	(4/4)

Rhythm Patterns & Hemiola

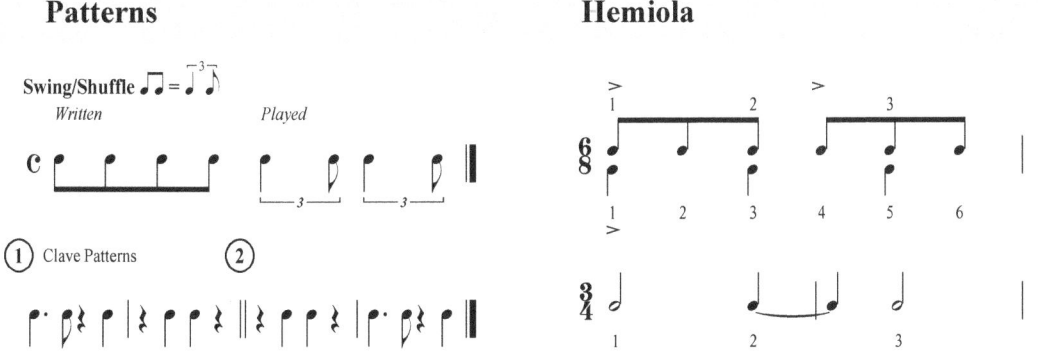

Music History Quick Reference

Ancient and Early Music (Before 800 CE)

- Music was part of daily life for storytelling, ritual, and ceremony.
- Early instruments included lyres, flutes, and hand drums.
- Greek philosophers studied sound and developed early modes.
- Music was not yet written down, so it was passed on by ear.

Medieval Music (c. 800–1400)

- The first written music appears with neumes that later evolve into notation.
- Gregorian chant becomes the foundation of early church music.
- Sung in Latin, usually in a single melodic line called monophony.
- By 1200, composers in Paris were experimenting with polyphony.
- The Ars Nova period introduces rhythmic notation and more complex structures.

Renaissance Music (c. 1400–1600)

- Composers develop polyphony where all voices are equal.
- Josquin (c. 1450-1521), Palestrina (c. 1525-1594), and Byrd (c. 1543-1623) create sacred and secular works.
- Madrigals and word painting connect emotion to text.
- Music printing allows composers to share their works widely.

Baroque Music (c. 1600–1750)

- Opera begins in Italy, blending music, poetry, and theatre.
- The basso continuo forms the harmonic base.
- Tonality becomes clear with major and minor keys.
- New composition forms appear, such as the fugue, suite, concerto, and oratorio.
- Notable composers include Bach (1685-1750), Handel (1685-1759), Vivaldi (1678-1741), and Purcell (c. 1659-1695).

"Music is the universal language of mankind." — Henry Wadsworth Longfellow

Music History Quick Reference

Classical Music (c. 1750–1820)

- The orchestra expands and becomes more balanced in sound.
- Common forms include the symphony, sonata, and string quartet.
- Melody with harmony expands (homophonic texture).
- Notable composers: Haydn (1732-1809), Mozart (1756-1791), and Beethoven (1770-1827).

Romantic Music (c. 1820–1900)

- Composers explore deeper expression and develop a personal style.
- Harmony expands with more chromatic tones and a wider dynamic range.
- National styles develop in Russia, Italy, Germany, and beyond.
- The piano becomes the main instrument at home.
- Composers: Chopin (1810–1849), Schumann (1810–1856), Liszt (1811–1886), Brahms (1833–1897), Wagner (1813–1883), Verdi (1813–1901), and Tchaikovsky (1840–1893).

Early 20th Century Music (c. 1900–1950)

- Debussy (1862–1918) and Ravel (1875–1937) contribute to impressionism.
- Stravinsky (1882–1971) experiments with rhythm and dissonance.
- Schoenberg (1874–1951) contributes to atonality and the twelve-tone method.
- Jazz emerges in the United States, influenced by blues and ragtime.
- Composers mix folk, classical, and new sound ideas.
- Recording technology and radio began to shape how people listen.

Late 20th Century and Modern Music (1950–Present)

- Musical boundaries dissolve and more styles blend together.
- Reich (b. 1936) and Glass (b. 1937) develop Minimalism.
- Electronic and digital tools introduce synthesizers and recorded samples.
- Popular styles such as rock, jazz, pop, hip hop, and world music evolve together.
- Film and game music bring orchestral sounds to new audiences.

"Where words fail, music speaks." — Hans Christian Andersen

Essential Music Glossary

I. General & Tempo Terms

Term	Symbol/Abbr.	Definition
Accelerando	accel.	Gradually get faster.
Adagio	–	Slow and calm tempo (slower than Andante).
A Tempo	–	Return to the original tempo.
Alla Breve	¢	Cut time (2/2 meter); half note gets the beat.
Allegro	–	Fast, lively tempo.
Andante	–	At a walking pace (moderate speed).
Lento / Largo	–	Very slow tempo (Largo is slower and broader).
Moderato	–	Moderate speed.
Rallentando	rall.	Gradually slow down.
Ritardando	rit.	Gradually slow down.
Rubato	–	Flexible tempo; expressive timing.
Vivace / Presto	–	Very fast and lively.

II. Dynamics & Expression

Term	Symbol/Abbr.	Definition
Crescendo	cresc. $\prec$	Gradually get louder.
Decrescendo	decresc. $\succ$	Gradually get softer.
Diminuendo	dim.	Gradually get softer.
Dolce	–	Sweetly, gently.
Espressivo	espr.	Expressively.
Forte	f	Loud.
Fortissimo	ff	Very loud.
Leggiero	–	Light, delicate.
Mezzo Forte	mf	Moderately loud.
Mezzo Piano	mp	Moderately soft.
Piano	p	Soft.
Pianissimo	pp	Very soft.
Sforzando	sfz	Sudden strong accent.
Subito	sub.	Suddenly (e.g., subito piano = suddenly soft).

III. Articulation & Style

Term	Symbol/Abbr.	Definition
Accent	>	Emphasis on a specific note or beat.
Articulation	–	The manner notes are performed.
Cantabile	–	In a singing style.
Fermata	𝄐	Hold the note or rest longer than written.
Legato	leg. ⌢	Smooth and connected notes.

Term	Symbol/Abbr.	Definition
Marcato	∧	Strongly accented or marked; often detached.
Simile	–	Continue in the same manner.
Solo	–	A single performer or part.
Staccato	•	Short and detached.
Tenuto	–	Hold the note for its full value; emphasized.
Tutti	–	Everyone plays together.

IV. Notation & Structure

Term	Symbol/Abbr.	Definition
Barline / Measure	–	Divides music into equal rhythmic units.
Clef	𝄞 𝄢 𝄡	Symbol defining pitch range.
Coda	⊕	A concluding section.
Da Capo	D.C.	Return to the beginning.
Dal Segno	D.S. 𝄋	Return to the 𝄋 symbol.
Fine	–	The end of a piece or section.
Key Signature	–	Sharps or flats defining the key.
Repeat Signs	𝄆 𝄇	Indicate a section to play again.
Slur	⌢	Connects notes smoothly (legato).
Tie	⌣	Connects two identical notes into one sound.
Time Signature	$\frac{4}{4}$ C	Numbers showing beats per bar and beat value.

V. Scales & Harmony

Term	Symbol/Abbr.	Definition
Dominant	5th	Chord built on 5th scale degree; often leads to tonic.
Enharmonic	–	Same note written differently (F♯-G♭).
Leading Tone	7th	7th scale degree; resolves to tonic.
Mediant	3rd	3rd scale degree.
Modulation	–	Change of key within a piece.
Parallel Major/Minor	–	Share the same tonic (C major / C minor).
Relative Major/Minor	–	Share the same key signature (C major / A minor).
Scale	–	Stepwise series of notes.
Subdominant	4th	4th scale degree.
Submediant	6th	6th scale degree.
Supertonic	2nd	2nd scale degree.
Tonality	–	Organizing pitches around a central pitch (tonic).
Tonic	1st	The "home" pitch of the key built on scale degree 1.
Tonicization	–	Briefly establishing a chord other than the tonic.
Transposition	–	Shifting music to another key keeping same intervals.
Voice Leading	–	Smooth movement of melodic lines between chords.

VI. Rhythm, Meter & Texture

Term	Symbol/Abbr.	Definition
Beat	–	The steady pulse of the music.
Consonance	–	Stable or pleasant sound.
Counterpoint	–	Independent melodic lines combined.
Dissonance	–	Tension or instability needing resolution.
Harmony	–	Notes sounding together.
Melody	–	The main tune or theme.
Meter	–	Organization of beats.
Ostinato	–	Repeating rhythmic or melodic figure.
Phrase	–	A musical "sentence" or unit of thought.
Polyrhythm	–	Two or more different rhythms simultaneously.
Rhythm	–	Pattern of sounds and silences.
Syncopation	–	Accenting offbeats or weak beats.
Texture	–	How parts combine (mono, homo, polyphonic).
Tuplet / Triplet	–	Division of notes into irregular groups.

VII. Performance & Technique

Term	Symbol/Abbr.	Definition
Arpeggio	–	Chord tones played one after another.
Cadence	–	Harmonic close of a phrase.
Cadenza	–	Solo passage, often virtuosic or improvised.
Glissando	*gl.* ⁄	Sliding smoothly between two pitches.
Improvisation	–	Creating or varying music spontaneously.
Pizzicato	*pizz.*	Plucked instead of bowed.
Sul Ponticello	–	Play near the bridge (brighter tone).
Sul Tasto	–	Play over the fingerboard (softer tone).
Sustain	–	To hold a note for its full value or longer.
Timbre	–	Tone color or quality of sound.
Tremolo	–	Rapid repetition of a note or interval.
Vibrato	*vib.* 〜	A rapid, slight wavering of pitch for warmth.

VIII. Common Foreign Terms

Term	Symbol/Abbr.	Definition
con brio	Ital.	With energy, spirited.
da capo	Ital.	From the beginning.
legato	Ital.	Smoothly connected.
staccato	Ital.	Detached, short.
timbre	Fr.	Tone color.
leitmotif	Ger.	Leading theme or motive.
cantus firmus	Lat.	Fixed melody.

CREATIVE TONES

Capture moments of musical inspiration, lyrics or lesson notes before they fade.

NOTES

Record important musical details here, from scales to composition ideas.

IDEAS & NOTES

IDEAS & NOTES

IDEAS & NOTES

IDEAS & NOTES

Other Book Titles From Kalymi Music

GUITAR

- The Blues Guitar Looper Pedal Book
- The Pop Rock Guitar Looper Pedal Book
- DADGAD Guitar Celtic Flatpicking
- Open D Guitar Celtic Flatpicking
- **Open G** Tuning Celtic Guitar Flatpicking
- Slide Guitar Collection
- Improve Your Guitar Chord Playing
- Guitar Blank Tablature & Reference
- Beginner Guitar Chord Book
- The Open D Guitar Christmas Songbook
- 101 Blues Riffs and Solos in Open D Guitar Tuning
- Classical Guitar Book in Open D Tuning
- Resonator Guitar Celtic Book
- 101 Blues Riffs and Solos in Open G Guitar Tuning

UKULELE

- Celtic World Collection - Ukulele
- Ukulele Blank Tablature Workbook & Reference
- The Ukulele Christmas Songbook
- Mastering Fingerstyle Ukulele
- Ultimate Ukulele Technique & Warm-Up Book

FIDDLE/VIOLIN

- Fiddle Tab Celtic Collection
- Fiddle Tab Traditional Collection
- Fiddle Tab Holiday Collection
- Easy Classical Violin Tabs

MANDOLIN/MANDOLA

- Celtic World Collection - Mandolin
- Mandolin Blank Tablature Workbook & Reference
- Mandolin Blues Book
- The Celtic Mandola Book (Treble and Alto Clef)

CIGAR BOX GUITAR

- Cigar Box Guitar Jazz & Blues Unlimited – 3-String
- Cigar Box Guitar Jazz & Blues Unlimited – 4-String
- Cigar Box Guitar – The Ultimate Collection - 2, 3 and 4-String
- Cigar Box Guitar – The Ultimate Collection Volume Two
- 101 Riffs and Solos for Four String Cigar Box Guitar
- 101 Riffs and Solos for Cigar Box Guitar
- Cigar Box Guitar Blues Overload
- The Complete Cigar Box Guitar Chord Book
- The Complete Cigar Box Guitar Chord Book 3-String
- The Complete Cigar Box Guitar Chord Book 4-String
- Celtic Collection 3 and 4-String
- Cigar Box Guitar Technique Book
- Cigar Box Guitar Classical Collection
- Cigar Box Guitar Holiday Collection
- 4-String Blank Tablature Workbook & Reference for Cigar Box Guitar
- 3-String Blank Tablature Workbook & Reference for Cigar Box Guitar

SHEET MUSIC ♪ *BOOKS* ♪ *POSTERS* ♪ *MUSIC GIFTS*

Online Store: brentrobitaille.com